T0062511

# Going Off-Center

## Observations from an At-Risk Teacher

DONNA PFANNENSTIEL

Abbott Press books may be ordered through booksellers or by contacting:

Abbott Press
1663 Liberty Drive
Bloomington, IN 47403
www.abbottpress.com
Phone: 1 (866) 697-5310



Scripture taken from the King James Version of the Bible.

ISBN: 978-1-4582-2177-3 (sc)
ISBN: 978-1-4582-2176-6 (e)

Library of Congress Control Number: 2018906974

Print information available on the last page.

Abbott Press rev. date: 6/15/2018

Dedicated to:

Bill Pfannenstiel—My husband of 42 years, who has always believed if I felt strongly about something I should go for it, and without waver, believing I would succeed in getting it. Thank you, darling…I love you.

# Acknowledgments

I am so grateful to so many people in my world; I hardly know where to begin; but, I will try.

John and Audra Durham (Blattel)—My parents. Thank you, for everything I am and for raising me to believe in myself. And, for always assuring me there is more good in the world than bad. Mom you told me I should write a book...and since you always do know what's best...here it is.

Erica, Karl, and Caleb McKimmey—Our daughter, son-in-law, and grandson. Thank you, Erica, for letting me use some of your stories and for teaching mommy many lessons through the years. Thank you, Karl, for the encouragement and for understanding that I *needed* to write this book. Thank you, Caleb, for getting it! And, for keeping my secret. My little trio, Thank you, for always being my inspirations in everything I do.

To my aunts and uncles—Colleen/Larry Waterman and Barbara/David Phillips for still allowing me to be a 'little' princess in the family. All of you have enriched my life in more ways than I can count. I love you all.

Cindy McIntyre—You led the way, and then supported me while I found my path. Thank you.

Janet Branch—You make me giggle like a little girl again, for that I will always be grateful. Thank you for your support.

Regina and Sara—The girls up-front. Both of you give so much support in so many ways...Thank you for your encouragement. I'm blessed to have the two of you in my world.

To all of my colleagues—I learn from each of you every day, and for that, I will always be grateful.

To Katri—Thank you so much. Love you.

# Contents

# 1 Beginning Again

"Do what you have to do...so you can do what you **want** to do."

In my early days as an educator, this phrase was posted in several prominent areas around my classroom. I thought I was very clever when I came up with these words of wisdom (even if they were grammatically incorrect), typed and mounted on colorful, eye-catching paper for my students, with wandering eyes, to read and to ponder. It was an effort to send a not-so-subtle message to my students; to do what must be done to meet the challenges of life; but, primarily to complete the lesson that lay before them. It resonated with some, others, not so much.

My name is Donna Pfannenstiel (Ms. Donna to my students), and I am in my 21st year as an educator in small-town U.S.A. I teach the Sciences in an alternative high school setting for At-Risk students. Sometimes I feel that I have become a little "Off Center." My center. Everyone has a center. That place where you are most comfortable. Preconceived notions of what is acceptable, rational, and what isn't. Due to my experiences as an At-Risk teacher my center has been moved. However; I have discovered it is not a wrong place to be, just different and for the most part I love it!

I started college later than most; at the ripe old age of 37 to become a teacher. It took me nearly ten years to earn an Associate of General Studies, a Bachelor of Science in Biology, a Masters in Education and my lifetime teaching certificate from the state of Missouri (it makes me tired just thinking about it).

Now during that time I wasn't just twiddling my thumbs. During the first three years of classes, I worked part-time at a local grocery store, continued to take care of my home, my husband of 18 years, our teenage daughter, and two cats. In turn, they took care of me; by not complaining when I had a paper due, and dinner was late or non-existent (except for the cats), helping with household chores, and pushing me out the door on those nights that I would have rather stayed home and skipped the class. (Yes, even teachers understand the desire to 'skip').

Having the support of your family is imperative. Making the decision to go back to school was a life-changing challenge; not just for me, but, for my family as well. It wasn't just about me going back to school, meeting new people, meeting deadlines, putting in the work to complete the assignments. It was also about me being absent from my family when sitting in those classes, having study sessions with those new people and needing solitude to write the papers and do the studying.

When I received my Associate's degree, I went to work as a paraprofessional in a new program for behavioral students, from the Junior High and High School. The premise of the program was that a student would go there, get fixed, (or so I was informed by one parent) and eventually return to the mainstream classroom. We'll discuss the reality of that actually happening later.

This brand new program was a stand-alone, separate from the mainstream population. And, I do mean 'stand-alone' literally. We were housed in a small building just off of the school grounds. It was my understanding, at the time, that this was a program designed, more or less, as the last chance for the students that would be enrolled there. These young people, for various reasons, could not be in a mainstream classroom. They needed special guidance, one-on-one involvement, and our population would be small. I won't lie...it was a scary prospect. The only paid jobs I had ever had was in retail, however; I'm a big believer in doing the hardest thing first, and the rest will be a piece of cake in comparison (I'm also a 'give me the bad news first' kind-of-gal). My decision, to take the job or not, was simple. I wanted to teach, and I wanted my foot-in-the-door with the district, so, I decided to take the job and said, "Thank You."

I was to work with two teachers and another para; student population yet to be decided. As it happened, I was the only female in the building for the first few months. The days were long with very few light moments. I saw behavior from some of the 'students' that I would not have believed had I not witnessed it for myself. I heard horror stories about the lives of my young charges, which, in turn, explained some of the behavior; however, that knowledge didn't make it any easier to deal with while in the moment. I came to realize that I was acquiring a new skill set as I maneuvered through my days. I was learning that I could run through a myriad of emotions rather quickly. I discovered that I could go from shocked and stunned- to pity and empathy- to struggling to understand and praying I would do and say the right thing for the student in the matter of a couple of minutes.

There were times when everything about my work-day felt surreal. When stepping through the door, of the two-room building, I would feel as if I was stepping inside of an M.C. Escher's lithograph. The one called *Relativity* comes to mind. At first glance, it appears to have multiple staircases leading its people to everywhere and nowhere at the same time. In actuality, it is a study of gravity from three different sources occupying the same spatial plane. That is what it felt like with a couple of the students. At any given time of the day, when I would survey the two small rooms, I felt as if these particular students were each caught by their own gravitational source and try as we might, there was no staircase for us to reach them. I felt sorry for the handful of our other students. For the most part, they tried; but, they had very little patience with those two. I couldn't fault them for that; they had issues of their own, and there was precious little time for us to focus on them. It seemed our energy was always directed elsewhere.

It took an open mind and an open heart to work there. It certainly wasn't what I had thought it would be; but, as everyone knows, very little in life turns out as the visual we create in our minds. I believe this was when I started to go a little off-center. In specific areas, I had to create a new normal. I had to learn to celebrate the small signs of progress. I had to start building my own staircase as it were. I was determined to see this through. I had made a commitment to myself and my family! I refused to let a few juveniles deter me from my goal. Did I mention some would call me stubborn? Although, I prefer to describe myself as tenacious.

The majority of the behaviors I witnessed I will not speak about here; however, there is one that I can describe. It was an unusual behavior that occurred regularly between some of the students. When separated during their lessons (on a computer-based program), one of them would make a 'cawing' sound, not exactly the call of a crow, but, similar. The next student from across the room would echo the sound. No one else appeared to be perturbed by this; but, I found it profoundly disturbing. I realize that probably sounds ridiculous to anyone reading this; yet, 21 years later I can still recall the painful, mournful sound. I suppose I could have had an overactive imagination, but I likened it to the sound of wounded animals calling to one another. When I mentioned this, 'wounded animal' scenario I had created in my head, to one of the teachers I was told very simply, "In a way they are."

Years later, upon reflection, I decided that one possible explanation for my preoccupation, with this one minor anomaly, was because I could not dwell on the other behaviors I had observed. The other behaviors were too overwhelming. And, I decided the teacher that I had spoke with was already a little off-center since this behavior was out-of-the-norm for a mainstream classroom; but, I wasn't there yet.

Nothing I had experienced in my own life and nothing I had been taught so far in college had prepared me for this. There were nights that I went home and cried; primarily, for my students (once in a while for myself), but, I hung in there, and I kept a running dialogue in my head with God. He most assuredly was listening, because about four months into the program we added a new student, a young girl, and as the only female educator in the building, she basically became my responsibility.

At times, when the emotional climate in the building became more intolerable than she could handle, she and I would go for a walk around the neighborhood that was just across the street; or, when the weather was good, we would sit outside on the front steps. She would talk—I would listen; keeping whatever judgments I had to myself. She taught me the importance of building a good relationship between the teacher and the student; long before I had heard of Ruby Payne. Occasionally, we would be joined by one or two of the other students along with my fellow para. These were the few moments when I and my fellow para could at least be a sounding board for our other students, and they could get a little reprieve from the tumultuous environment that was.

Finally, along with the month of May came the last day of the school year. "Woo-Hoo! I did it!" By saying "I did it" I mean somehow I had survived (didn't quit) and miraculously so had my dream of teaching. I still wanted my own classroom. My superiors told me that I had 'done a great job', and they asked if I would like to work in the MR room at the Junior High the next year?

First of all, when they told me I 'had done a great job', I translated this to mean, "Wasn't it remarkable that at no point had she went running and screaming out of the building?" Don't laugh...I had heard, from a reliable source, that at some point the next year that either, the teacher or the para, did go running and screaming out of the building. Perhaps, not the screaming part, but, there was definitely some speed walking involved, and I'm confident he or she went back later.

Second, our MR room, what is now called ID (Intellectually Disabled), serviced students with IQ's between 50 to 70 and was housed in the main building of the Junior High. The students had core classes in math and English with a Special Education (SPED) teacher. If I agreed, I would be her para, and I was to 'shadow' certain students when attending their other classes (also known as push-in) along with assisting the SPED teacher in her classroom. This sounded more like a regular classroom setting, and I was eager to have the experience; I was also anxious **not** to return to my previous assignment. So when asked if I wanted to work in the MR room...I accepted and said, "Bless You."

Don't get me wrong; I do not regret working in the behavioral unit. During my time there I learned many lessons that would serve me well later in my career. On a personal level, I had learned to have a genuine appreciation for the good things in my life, both past and present. I had always felt privileged to have a wonderful childhood. I actually knew I was lucky as a youngster. I am an only child; for which I would 'Thank' my parents frequently and sincerely; usually after spending time with my friends and *their* siblings. I was then and to this day, grateful for kind, loving, supportive parents; they liked me, and I liked them. They were always my parents first and my friends second. You see, in my sheltered life, of not only, great parents but: grandparents, aunts, and uncles, it never occurred to me there was an option as to whether or not a family displayed love, respect, and loyalty; it just was. Over the years, in my career, I have looked at some of my students after hearing their stories and asked myself; "How do they do it? How do they show up to school at all? What makes them return my smile with one of their own?" I've been told that 'young people are resilient'; and there must be some truth to that; but, I'm not sure I would have been that strong, at that age, without the protection and love my parents and family provided. My appreciation for my life and my family...is something I have never taken for granted again. God has blessed me.

On a professional level I learned that I did not want, nor, could

I handle working in a behavioral unit again; yet, I also knew I had received an invaluable education in my first year. A note about the young lady that I mentioned before; we had built a good rapport in our months together, and over the years, from time to time, she would contact me to talk when there was something, good or bad, happening in her life. I had made a connection, a difference in at least one student's life and that made a difference to me.

I had studied "Nature vs. Nurture" on the pages of my pysch textbooks; but, during my first professional assignment, I had real-life examples that could not be duplicated in any college classroom. Regardless, of everything that I had been through; and all I had witnessed; I had weathered it through and I was still there. My first year with the district had afforded me what I really wanted: my-foot-in-the-door.

# 2 Foot-in-the-Door

I am not sure the Special Education teacher that I worked with would describe her classroom (grades 7-9) as a haven, but, I surely did. Whereas, the negative emotional climate and stress levels of my previous assignment were at the highest end of the spectrum, in her classroom, they were virtually non-existent.

If I were to create a Venn diagram of the behavioral unit vs. the SPED classroom, I would find very little that would overlap. Where academics was forced to feel like an afterthought in the unit *(due to my "wounded animals");* it was of paramount importance in her room. In my previous assignment, the lessons were regulated to a computer program; but, in her room, we worked directly with the students, both in group and one-on-one. Where chaos was the norm in the unit, order reigned in the SPED room. Not only order, but, organization, compassion, empathy, appreciation, and insight. The SPED instructor (now retired) was a wonderful teacher, not only to her students but, to me as well. I could not have had a better mentor.

For two years I was her para, and I am grateful for that experience. It was from her that I first heard, *"What is fair is not always equal and what is equal is not always fair."* In other words, sometimes it is necessary to level the playing field for those that are academically, emotionally challenged, or both. These children (I began to think of them as "my kids") were so endearing, so sweet that in the beginning, I tended toward wanting to be a mother-figure first and to be a teacher second. My mentor never criticized me. Instead, she allowed me to learn through observing her interactions with the students. It soon became apparent that I had to be a teacher first for the sake of our kids. They needed, maybe more than others, to reach their full potential. It was from her that I learned to expect everything they could do, push for their maximum; but, to never push for things they would never be capable of doing. A lesson that I still carry with me today.

I found it extraordinary when I would hear a few of the teachers complain about the special accommodations that needed to be made for these children. I thought perhaps it was the inequity between a SPED room and a regular classroom. Maybe there was a little resentment associated with the system. After all, these teachers had 20 plus different students in their classrooms six times per day and no extra help; while the SPED class had the same 13 students all day and had a full-time helper. *But, what's fair isn't always equal.* Yet, there was something else, something more I had also noticed about a few of these disgruntled teachers. Some of them appeared to be very ill-at-ease around our students. I didn't understand that. For the most part, these children were exceptionally well behaved. From my observations, they were far better behaved, more polite than many of the students at the Junior High. The students that didn't need the services of Special Education.

I did not exist in a bubble, but, I had been raised by extremely tolerant people. My parents had always taught me that we were all only one head injury or illness from being similarly afflicted as the students that I now served. Paraphrasing along the lines of the old proverb, taken from Corinthians, my parents would tell me: "There, but by the Grace of God goes you or someone you know and love. How would you want them to be treated? How would you want to be treated?"

I had heard the derogatory terms and had seen people that would skirt around or shy away from people that are mentally challenged. Frankly, I had always, privately, associated these behaviors with ignorance. Therefore, imagine my surprise when I witnessed this type of behavior (from a few) out of a group of people that was not only well educated; but, trained to educate. After witnessing one particular incident, that I didn't like, by a specific teacher; I approached my mentor with my observations one afternoon as we stood just outside her door. We were in-between classes monitoring the hallway, waiting for the tardy bell to signal the beginning of the next class. Unfortunately, my revelation did not take her by surprise.

With a sad little smile and a small shrug of her shoulders she said; "For whatever reason, some people are not comfortable around the mentally challenged."

"But these are highly educated people who chose to work with children," I argued.

"I know," she replied, "but a school faculty is simply a microcosm of the world."

I can remember looking past her observing our kids, that was already in the room. They were in various stages of preparing for class. As I grappled with this new insight...I hurt for them. If they couldn't find complete support and tolerance here...then where? Eventually, through working with these children, I began to realize they had a particular capability that I hadn't been aware of before in the mentally challenged. I began to believe that although they struggled (and always would) with learning, that God had given them something to compensate for that struggle. The capacity to cut through the platitudes and the thinly veiled ridicule they endured. I could see the hurt after a 'joke' had been made at their expense. I could also see a firming of the jaw, a straightening of the shoulders, and a hardening look in their eyes. I even had one child to catch my eye and shake her head 'no' in an almost imperceptible movement toward me when I was about to call another student down for their crude behavior on her behalf. She knew what I didn't; not only would my reprimand make it worse, but, she would be embarrassed also. They knew who respected them and who did not. Just because they were academically mentally challenged didn't mean they were ignorant.

In the two years, I had spent "shadowing" I can think of only one child (out of 13) who was also labeled BD, Behavioral Disorder (now known as ED-Emotional Disorder), that was ever 'called on the carpet' for discipline. For the most part, these children, worked very hard at their lessons, giving you everything they had. To those that were and to those that are "uncomfortable"... in my opinion, you really missed out. Those children were among the most polite, loving, generous, and sweet-natured people, I have ever met. Those children enriched my life.

Despite what others may have thought, I knew I was working in a great classroom with an excellent mentor and terrific children. I, also, had the added bonus, when shadowing certain students, of observing numerous Junior High teachers in regular classroom settings; this was an education in itself.

These teachers were all veterans, and each had their own style. Some were a little laid-back, while others were more structured. I was able to compare and contrast not only their methods but their classroom management techniques. I became an unobtrusive, quiet fixture in the room. This allowed me to observe first-hand what worked and when the teacher's back was turned, those things that didn't work with the students.

I truly admired the high energy of one teacher in particular. He seemed to be constantly in motion, moving from one student to another, moving from the front of the room to the back, involving each one in the lesson. He captured their attention and their imagination. His enthusiasm was contagious, and he drew me into his lessons also.

One day, after a particularly exuberant session I jokingly asked, "How tired are you at the end of the day?"

With a big smile, he replied, "Pretty pooped some days, those are the days I know I did a good job. I feed off of their energy."

It would be a few years into the future before I would be able to truly relate to what he was saying. It took teaching my own classes to understand that euphoric feeling of watching the dawning of a concept on the face of a student. That "I get it" moment and eagerness to learn more is a true motivator for a teacher.

I sat-in on Social Studies classes, Science, Music, Exploratory classes, and a Home Economics Class. I must say the teachers in those classes seemed to appreciate my presence and they were good to my kids.

I have to laugh about the Home Ec class; not about the class, but, about my initial reaction to the Home Ec teacher. You see, the teacher in that class was *my* Home Ec teacher when I was in Junior High. She was so young then. Upon reflection, I realized she must have been in her first or second year of teaching at that time, and I must have been among some of her first students. All I know is that even though I was an adult and working for the school district, she still had a hold over me... when she said, "Get quiet and sit down!" I was the first one in the room to shut my mouth and find a seat.

# 3 "Do you want to be a teacher?"

In May of 2000, I earned my Bachelor of Science degree in Biology. I chose not to attend my graduation ceremony in 2000; however, I did drive to the campus, picked-up my degree and celebrated by having dinner out with my family.

I had attended my graduation ceremony for my Associate's Degree in 1997. Why was that ceremony more important to me than my Bachelor's ceremony? Because, the associate's degree was my first significant milestone in reaching my original goal. I needed to take that moment and acknowledge my accomplishment. It was important. That degree provided options. It would allow me to apply for a Paraprofessional position or at the very least apply to be a substitute teacher. At that time, I had walked across the stage with the knowledge of knowing I could do this and a resolve that I would do this. My Associate's Degree afforded me with the opportunity to have a glimpse of the world to which I wanted to become a part. It brought me to where I am now. Looking back at that time, I realized I could have stopped there. I had a job I loved as para; but, in my heart, I knew I would not be satisfied until I stood in front of my students in my own classroom. So I pressed on.

Actually, during the last semester of earning my Bachelors Degree in Biology, I was concurrently taking classes that would count towards a Master's in Education degree. I was still a little way from fulfilling the additional criteria to get what I was really after: a Missouri Teaching Certificate. Since my paper chase had a ways to go; why not go for the Master's degree also? So I didn't go to my Bachelor's graduation ceremony. In a somewhat quirky way, I felt like I had already moved past that. Besides, without the state certification, all of the degrees in the world wouldn't allow me to say "I am a teacher." Or, so I thought.

At some point, shortly after having completed my Bachelors Degree I received a message that one of our district Superintendents wanted me to contact his office. This particular Super was the head of Human Resources. Ironically, he had been my American History teacher when I was a Junior in High School; not to mention, that he had also been one of my university instructors.

I can remember calling my mom in a kind of panic, "Good grief, have I done something wrong? I can't imagine why he wants to see me."

"Donna, he is going to offer you a teaching job," she replied.

"No, no, that can't be it. I have so far to go before I get my certificate. Maybe he is going to fire or replace me." I answered.

She just laughed.

Another lesson learned one I really should have already known: Never argue with momma; cause momma is always right! Sure enough, minutes after being ushered into his office, he offered me a teaching position! Remember that newly acquired skill set that I spoke of earlier? The capability of running through a set of emotions rather quickly came in handy while he sat at his desk and I sat facing him. *Relief,* I wasn't being replaced or fired. *Shock,* of being offered a job for which I had not applied, nor, did I know existed. *Fear,* from that old standard, sudden lack of confidence. What if I can't do it? Am I ready? I'm not ready. I haven't had time to process this turn of events. But, mostly *confusion,* how was this possible? He must have me confused with someone else.

I'm fairly confident all of the above was revealed racing across my face. One thing I know with certainty about myself is that I would make a lousy poker player or con artist. Whatever I am thinking or feeling I wear it on my face for all to see; if you know me well enough to read it. Judging by the bemused expression of the gentleman across the desk he knew me well enough.

I found myself nearly arguing with the head of H.R. "I can't. I'm not done. I don't have a certificate, just my Biology Degree and my Biology Praxis (a test that all teachers must pass in their field or they don't teach)." Side-note: It's probably not a good idea to argue your qualifications with H.R. when you are being offered a job. At this point, he took pity on me and explained about the 'Provisional Teaching Certificate.' What I primarily understood from his explanation was, that as long as I continued with my schooling to fulfill the criteria needed for a Permanent Teaching Certificate, the district could petition the state for an emergency provisional and I could start teaching now. Wow! Who knew? I certainly didn't. To this day I find it extraordinary that I had spent all this time with university advisers, instructors, and had been a para working in a school district for three years, and yet, this was the first time I had heard about a Provisional Certificate. It took me a moment to process this piece of information. It began to sink in that this wasn't some sort of mistake. He didn't have me confused with someone else. He was serious. When I think back on it now, it's kind of embarrassing. I mean, really? Why I ever thought that a person in his position would not know precisely what he was doing, still mystifies me.

So, I finally found my tongue enough to ask what I thought was the most logical of questions: "What position are you offering me?"

"It's a new program," he enthused. "The alternative school. Have you heard anything about it? You would be the Science teacher."

Oh Boy!!! I had been part of a new program before. Yes, I had heard a few things about it, and the speculations sounded ominous. Most people thought it would be a dumping ground for behavioral students. The first program, the behavioral unit, the one I had been assigned to in my first year, was in it's last few days. It had had a three-year run and it would sunset on the last day of this school year. Word was, the new program would be a replacement for it on a larger scale. My stomach dropped. I couldn't do that again. I alluded to the scuttlebutt that was going around. He assured me that was not the case. He also sent me to speak with the Special Services Superintendent as this would fall under her domain. I had a professional relationship with her as she was the Director of all paras in the district, and I had taken more than one class at university under her tutelage. She, too, assured me this new program was nothing like the first. It was specifically designed to address the district's drop-out rate; a task she had been assigned. I would be working with At-Risk students. (An At-Risk student is one that is at risk of failing and/or dropping out before graduating). Students that would be serious about their education and focused on graduating. The student population would be relatively small and focused on credit recovery. Also, due to a unique aspect of the new program, BD students would not be eligible for enrollment. That caught my interest.

I was told to think it over and let them know. I drove home in a daze. I could realize my dream of having my classroom much sooner than I had thought was possible. Of course, I would still have to continue my own schooling, but, I didn't have to wait for some far away, fuzzy, future date or sweat out one interview after another trying to get a teaching job. I could have one now. I could start living my goal in a few short summer months. I talked to my husband. I talked to my daughter. I talked to my mom. I talked to myself, "Don't mess this up, Donna. This is what you have been working for...for a few years now." About an hour later I called Central Office and spoke to the District's H.R. secretary.

"Yes, I will take the position," I announced clearly into the phone with more bravado than I was actually feeling.

She laughed and asked, "Was there ever any doubt?"

Hmmm...was there any doubt? Of course, there was some doubt. I would still be going to school at night, and although, I had been working full-time for the past three years and attending classes at night, I would now have the full responsibilities of a teacher. I would be leaving an area that I loved, and would be sad to leave. I wondered if I knew enough. I was confident in my knowledge of the subject matter, but, some self-doubt crept into my head. I had to convey that knowledge, and I had yet to take all of my teaching classes.

I can remember discussing my self-doubt with my mom, and I still remember what she said, "Well, apparently, there are two Superintendents that know you and believe you are ready. You didn't ask for this; they came to you."

I had not thought about it in that manner. I suddenly felt very humbled and resolved. I would not let the Superintendents, my family, or myself down. I would do this. Both feet were in the door now.

Thank you, mom.

# 4 The New Program—First Year

When meeting people for the first time, among the most commonly asked questions are: "What do you do?" "Where do you work?" Upon answering that I am a teacher, the next question they ask is: "Which school do you work in?" This is where it gets tricky. When I respond with the alternative high school, I receive looks of pity and an "Oh," of sympathy. All they had heard, apparently, was the word 'alternative.' Most people automatically equate 'alternative' with 'bad.' I would be told that "You must be a saint" or "You must be an angel." Oh if they only knew. I do my best; but, I'm a far cry from either saint or angel.

I have learned to laugh it off and say "Oh I don't know about that. You might want to ask my students. They might disagree."

With a small shake of my head, I tell them, "It's not what you think. I love my job most days." They will then look at me as if I have lobsters crawling out of my ears.

It is at this moment that I say, "It isn't a traditional alternative school."

Then they want an explanation. I am always happy to talk to people about our school; however, if it is the checker at the local discount store that is doing the asking, the people in line behind me are not always interested in listening to my answer. Ever notice how cranky people can get when they're waiting in line?

So my short answer has become, "We are a credit recovery unit, not a behavioral unit."

Poof! Lobsters disappear.

I'm not really happy with that answer either; we are so much more, and with that in mind (and since this is my story) I am going to explain my understanding of what the program was always meant to be.

First, it was the brain-child of a handful of, in my opinion, very progressive educators. As I mentioned before it was meant to be a credit recovery unit. You know, for those young people that would drop-out for varying reasons. Or, for those that missed so much school, their credits had been pulled. Some wanted to work or needed to work. It was built for those that were just sick of traditional school; only to discover they couldn't get very far without, at the bare minimum, a high school diploma. There is absolutely nothing wrong with working in fast food eateries. It's honest work and personally, when I roll-up to the window for the occasional burger and fries, I want someone on the other side. But, flipping burgers is a hard way to make a living, unless, you're the one that owns the local franchise or you're the manager.

As I said before, this is a small city with only one high school; albeit, a rather fully populated high school. I believe the enrollment is generally around 1300-to-1500 students give or take. Our main high school campus is nice, but, hallways can get very crowded very quickly. Some people are uncomfortable to the extreme in any crowd and simply cannot function in a crowd. Then, there are those that cannot sit still for the 90 minute classes (block system). Some people need more one-on-one instruction than others or constant attention and reassurance. Some students simply need a little extra time to complete an assignment. That can be a difficult task for a regular classroom teacher with 25 plus students. We were built for the students that need something a little different. We were built for that square peg that refuses to be whittled down into a round peg in order to fit. We were never meant to be a traditional alternative school. We were never meant to be a behavioral unit.

The new program was to have no more than 10 students per class. I was one of four academic teachers. A 1:10 teacher- to- student ratio is considered optimal for an alternative school setting, you can check any informational article on the net. The number of teachers dictated our population to be no more than 50 enrolled. This program was to address the various issues and concerns with current students in danger of giving-up or returning students that had already given-up, ages 16 to 21; which in turn would lower our districts drop-out rate.

Second, we also had another component that set our school apart from the average alternative school; a work component. Our students would be receiving factory work training as part of their daily schedule. The work was supplied from outsourcing by various supportive businesses and factories from around town. They would receive a paycheck and earn credit. The weekly paychecks were stopped a few years ago and were replaced with all-paid field trips. Some are purely educational, and all are for experiences that many of our students would not otherwise have. The field trips also give the teachers and students a chance to interact in a less structured environment. To my knowledge, eighteen years later, we are still the only alternative school with this type of work element incorporated in our curriculum. This was the unique component that would not allow behavioral students to participate in this particular program, as I had been told earlier by the Superintendents. Think what you may, but, I had seen proof positive that it is not a wise choice to put such items as hammers, drills, saws, etc., into the hands of a BD student.

Our program was credit recovery biased; therefore, the classes were streamlined and shortened to 35 minute blocks. What did this mean to the students? It meant that even if they didn't like a particular subject they only had to sit through it for 35 minutes a day and then be off to another class. It also meant that with only four academic teachers plus the work component they would undoubtedly have more than one class each day with every teacher. Plus, they would receive more credits per year (providing they passed the classes) than from the main campus.

What did this mean to the teachers? First, it meant that we needed to get to know our students and build a strong rapport with each of them. We would be working with them on a rather intense basis multiple times per day. It also meant 40 class preps per week. That's right 40! I, along with my academic colleagues, taught eight *different* classes per day. I taught, Biology, Ecology, Earth Science, Botany, Anatomy, Genetics, and all four of us had a Work Ethics class. That left me with one more block to fill. It was suggested that I could teach a modified Chemistry class. Chemistry? But, honestly, what I could teach, with any authority in Chemistry, would take approximately four weeks. What would I teach for the other eight months? I was reminded of a short conversation I had one day early on as a push-in para with the Earth Science teacher:

"Have you read the news about the genetic conundrum with those twins that was just born?" I asked.

"Genetics? Oh no, no, no. I'm a rock man." He answered.

At the time I laughed. He had made his declaration with such a sense of sincerity; but, when it was suggested that I could teach Chemistry, I sincerely understood what he had been saying.

I am a life science teacher. Humans, critters, and daisies. I had to come up with something different. The really great thing was—they let me! I was rather surprised by this turn of events. I recalled talking to my daughter one day several years before, about some of her classes; and I remember telling her I had a few ideas for creating some new classes:

"Oh mom, I don't think they let teachers do that unless they have been there for years," she informed me. "Certainly not before they're tenured. The whole thing has to align with the state, the curriculum...be approved by the board." She then went on to tell me about one of her teachers that had been trying to form a new class for years, with no luck.

Well, that was disappointing to hear. Of course at the time I didn't know that I would be helping and working to build a new program; nor, did I know that the people who were heading it up would be thrilled that I was, "… embracing this new territory with such enthusiasm." In other words; they gave me the green light. It was unexpected, but, I couldn't have been happier. I went back to that conversation with my daughter and pulled an idea I didn't think they would reject. I created a class I named Missouri Natural Science. I designed the curriculum, matched it to Missouri's Standards and Goals, gathered the materials I needed to teach it, wrote the lectures, created the class worksheets, projects, and tests. It was board approved and added to the curriculum. I was thrilled. Not only did I get to teach sooner than I thought was possible, but I was allowed a creative outlet. But, most importantly, I didn't have to teach Chemistry. And that was worth every extra hour I worked on weekends and nights writing my class.

I still teach Missouri Natural Science. It's a combination of a little Missouri history, a little Missouri geography, and a study of indigenous Missouri wildlife ranging from reptiles and amphibians to mammals and birds. As I explain to my students every year; "You're sitting in the middle of this state. You may not always live in Missouri, but, you're here now. Why not learn a little something about it?"

It would be remiss of me not to tell you about our first few weeks and the building we were housed in for 16 years. It might explain a few things along the way. The building was an old flat-roofed factory located within walking distance of the main high school campus. It was on the small side, and a portion of the structure was partially underground like a basement. There were no windows in the classrooms. It had a dock and work area, necessary for the work component of the program and enough space to be cordoned-off into small classrooms (mine was the smallest). It also had a tiny kitchen where, starting in our second year, the teachers would serve the lunch fetched from the main campus in insulated front loading food pan carriers. (Incidentally, 18 years later and nothing has changed on that front). Eventually, GED (Adult education) classes would be held (separate area) in our building, and it would also house the district's print shop. Area businesses had been quite generous in donating furniture and funds to refurbish the building. Some of the renovations were completed by students from the Vocational classes giving them hands-on experience.

However, when the first day of school came in the year 2000, our building had yet to be completed. Five teachers, one part-time administrator and 22 students (19 boys and three girls) began what we fondly called the *Magic School Bus* rides. That's right, while we waited for our building to be completed we were on a bus touring every local factory that would have us within a 50- mile radius. It was like being on a field trip every day...**for two weeks**. The novelty wore off for the students about 10:45 a.m. on the third day. For my colleagues and me, it wore off about 10:45 on the second day.

From the first day I tried to view this new program as a wild, and hopefully, wonderful ride, (preferably, we would not continue to be so literal on the ride part). If not wild and wonderful, at the very least, never dull. Our goals were clear. To put it succinctly we were to: get them in, get them caught up on credits, and get them back to the main campus to graduate. That last one didn't last long. The teachers, principals, and superintendents 'got schooled' by the students on that one...they wouldn't leave! At the end of the first year, we had a few students that had earned enough credits, to continue with their classes on the main campus. The majority of the students didn't want to go back. They wanted to graduate from the credit recovery program.

Even though that wasn't the original plan; I suppose we should look at it as a testimony that we were doing something right. There was an interview process for each student to be accepted into the program. Everyone was upfront about the goals of the school.

They agreed to attend this school with the knowledge that when they had earned the needed credits they would return to the main campus. We asked for some clarification from the students, and the following are some of the reasons that I remember that they gave:

- I'm doing good here, and I don't want to go back. I'll quit.
- I feel like you guys really care, and I won't go back. I'll quit.
- I'm doing good here, cuz you guys help us. I'll quit before I go back.
- I feel like you guys are family. I'll quit today if I can't stay here.
- I can't go back there....I"ll just quit school.

As you can see there was a pattern forming. They kinda had our hands tied. If we forced them to leave and they did quit, that would defeat our whole purpose. So we adjusted our thinking. They were given the option of going back if they so desired. If a smaller class size, shortened stream-lined curriculum and an abundance of help when warranted wasn't enough, then apparently, we were not what they needed. If students are not successful with us, they can always go back. However, in the beginning, staying, was a little more iffy and had to be agreed upon by the teachers as well as the students. If a smaller class size, shortened stream-lined curriculum and an abundance of help wasn't helping with their credit recovery, then they were not taking advantage of the program...they were taking advantage of us. That's how it was; that's not necessarily how it is now.

One thing, which I feel we have always battled, is that kids get the idea they will have very little if any school work. Just like the adults I spoke of earlier in this chapter having preconceived notions about the type of students we serve when they hear the word *alternative*, many of our new- to- us students also carry preconceived ideas of our alternative school program. For example, some seem to think that just by gracing us with their presence should be enough to pass a class,and sometimes their presence is rather sporadic. There are those that come to us thinking that it will be so-o-o much easier than the mainstream classes they are currently attending (or, as the case may be, not attending). They think there won't be much in the way of classroom work; if any at all, and that regular rules won't apply. To clarify the difference between their slightly distorted idealism and the reality of what they have walked into, I will speak to each 'notion' separately.

Attendance is the basis of their grade in our work component (shop). We also have daily grades in each class that are based on attendance and attentiveness (more about that later in the book).

Hopefully, classes are easier because the teacher to student ratio is one to ten. Classes might be considered easier due to the shortened length. Much of what students consider to be busywork is eliminated; making the work they are given very important to their grades. We normally do not assign homework since we, the teachers, do not go home with them. Also, many of our students have after-school jobs, a few have children to care for, and some don't know where they will lay their heads at night on any given day. For some at-risk students, homework gives them another way to fail.

Our rules may actually appear much tighter than on the main campus because we are so small. Students can't get by with much simply due to the size of our population and the size of the building. There aren't too many places to hide, and the shenanigans are not easily hidden in a crowd of fifty.

It generally comes as a great shock to them to learn that although we are an 'alternative' school—we are not an alternative *to* school. School is still school; we are all about that 'reading, writing, and arithmetic; with science and history thrown in for good measure.

# 5 "We don't need no stinkin' rules!"

## (But secretly we want them)

Rules and expectations. Every teacher has them. Due to seniors leaving at semester (having earned their credits), and new students starting, (now that we have space), I start every semester off with a reading of them. Can you hear the moans and groans? Students always act as if they don't want to hear anything about rules, but, the reality is they really do want them, and they want you to uphold them. In my experience, what they don't want is for you to lie to them or what they perceive as a lie. Young people, in general, take a very black or white—wrong or right view of the world; there doesn't seem to be much in the way of gray areas.

When I took my 'teaching classes' at the university, they would talk about creating our classroom rules and expectations. They would also talk a lot about consequences, good and bad. We were introduced to several different methods on the writing of classroom rules. We would be tasked with a project on writing our own rules and the mechanics of classroom management. Normally, by the time you have reached this stage you have had at least some exposure to real classrooms. Many of us were working in schools in some capacity. They would tell us to look at the sweetest kid in the room. Now imagine imposing our rules and the consequences for breaking those rules on that child; make no mistake that's a tough one.

Another method is 'letting the children set the consequences' for the rules the children created. The driving force behind this method is giving some ownership and control to the students. That may work for some in a regular classroom. Perhaps, in my opinion, this method is suited best to a younger population; but, I wouldn't advise using it for teenaged At-Risk.

I tell my students, "This is my classroom, and you are my guests. I always want my guests to be comfortable and to feel welcome; but, I also expect my guests to treat me, my home, and my other guests with respect."

In my experience and through my observations these children have been given or forced, to take too much control in their lives already. So many of them, for various reasons, have had to make grown-up decisions long before they were grown-up. They are tired of picking up the slack for an absentee mother, father, or both. Keep in mind that absenteeism can take different forms. A parent does not have to be literally absent from the home to be absent from the relationship.

Everything I was taught was excellent information with statistics to back it up. To give real thought and to visualize how I wanted my classroom to run was good. To practice writing it out and receiving feedback from knowledgeable instructors was great! You know what's coming next, right? A 'But…'.

But, I learned the most important rule for my classroom and the basis of my future student-teacher relationships from my daughter, long before I decided to be a teacher. I can't remember exactly how old she was; maybe 8th or 9th grade. We were in our kitchen, she was sitting at the breakfast bar, and I was puttering about with something. We were talking about some of her classes and how things were going at school. As the conversation meandered, I asked about one particular class that she had been so excited to attend. To be honest, I can't remember which class it was or the teacher's name; but, I will never forget the disgust in her voice as she spoke of the teacher for that class. To say I was taken aback would be putting it mildly;

"I thought you really liked her..." I interjected.

"Oh she's alright, but, I thought she was going to be different; but, she isn't. She's just like all the rest of them," she said.

Color me intrigued.

"What are you talking about?" I asked.

"Well at the first of the year she went over her rules like they all do. She made a big deal about how she wouldn't put up with any nonsense," she said.

At this point I smiled, my little girl was a good kid, we had never been called to the office for her behavior, she never spent a day in ISS that I'm aware of and we couldn't complain about her grades.

"She said she would write us up the first time if we broke her rules. There was something about the way she said it. I *believed* her."

Oh boy!

"Got some rough kids in the class?"

"Yeah. They break the rules all the time, and she has not written any of them up. She just threatens them with *next time* over and over again."

"Are they bothering you?"

"Well, not me personally. It's just that I like the subject, and she had some fun ideas, but, they're ruining it, and they don't get in trouble like she said they would."

Hesitantly, I asked, "So you don't really respect her like you did?"

"Well no," she replied emphatically. "Basically, she lied. I can't respect her if I can't believe her."

Whoa!

I couldn't really say anything to her. As her father and I had been raised, so was she. My husband and I had taught her to have a strong sense of right and wrong. She was simply parroting what we had always told her. She had been taught that at the end of the day all anyone has is their word. Break that, and you don't have anything. We had taught her that if she wanted to have a voice, wanted to be heard; if she wanted trust and respect, then she had to be honest and keep her word. Otherwise, why would anyone listen or believe her about anything?

When I sat down to write my rules, I kept that conversation in my mind. I knew whatever my rules were to be if I wanted the respect of my students I would have to follow through with the consequence the first time a rule was broken.

With that in mind, here is my advice. Whether you are in a mainstream classroom with two or three At-Risk students or a school for At-Risk—DON'T try to bluff. There will always be at least one that will test you...ALWAYS. I have been tested on the first day of school. Be aware; the other students will also be watching, to see if you keep your word. Talk of your reaction will spread among the population quickly because kids live for this stuff; the drama. Whatever you do will set a precedent for your reputation among the students immediately. Let's say you decide to cut some slack with the first rule breaker with a *'next time...'* because you're tired, you don't feel like a confrontation, you don't want to start or end your day with a hoopla, you don't want to do the paperwork, call the parents, etc. All perfectly understandable reasons. But, let's follow you're *'next time'* through to the next time, because, make no mistake, there will be a next time. The next time may not be the same student, but, now every student will expect the same treatment. They will expect a free pass with a *"next time'*. So let's say instead you do decide to get tough with the next rule breaker, expect to hear the (proverbial) scream. It will be long and loud about how "you don't like me, you're not being fair, *Johnny* did it too, and you didn't punish him." Suddenly you may find yourself blustering in defense of your actions to a teenage kid. If you're not careful, you may place yourself at their level arguing with them. Not a good place to be. And, I speak from experience. If you don't want to find yourself in this position rip the bandage off quickly...give Johnny the consequences you promised in the first place, the first time.

Now that you have doled out the consequence the first time, BE CONSISTENT! Consistency, this is something that I don't think they pushed hard enough in my teaching classes. Your rules must be observed for everyone, every day, all day. Unless, you want to run-the-risk of becoming known as that teacher that never punishes the ones she/he likes and always punishes the ones she/he doesn't like, consistency is crucial. Your students may not always like it, but, I genuinely believe it makes them feel safer, and more secure in the knowledge they can count on you one way or the other.

You will find a copy of my expectations later in this book. It has taken me several years to hone them into something that works for me. Notice that I don't ask them to agree with my rules before signing on the bottom line; just that they acknowledge their understanding of them. However, there are always those individuals that want to challenge any rule. This is some of the grumblings and complaining that I have received for religiously adhering to my rules and my word:

"I forgot."
"I didn't think that's what it meant."
"You should give me another chance...it's not fair."
"I didn't mean to do it."
"None of the other teachers care about me doing this."
"I was just kidding around."

My answer is always the same:

"I don't lie. I told you what would happen and I kept my word. I have a piece of paper with your signature that says you understood my expectations and understood the consequences if those expectations were not met."

I have had students to tell me, "Oh, I just signed that thing, I didn't pay any attention to what you said." I love it when they come up with that one.

My reply: "Well, you have learned two things today. First: that

I keep my word and second: a wonderful life lesson. Never sign anything that you don't read and understand." For me that's the end of the argument, I'm done. Consequences are carried out.

Believe it or not this 'first time' - 'all the time' (hard-line) method can be the first building block to a good relationship and rapport with many of your students. Case in point; below is a note that a recent graduate (had been with us for two years) handed to me before leaving (Name removed for privacy):

"MRS DONNA,

I REALLY LOVE THAT YOU DON'T TAKE ANYONE'S B.S.

YOU'RE A REAL ROLE MODEL. KEEP YOUR HEAD UP AND STAY STRONG GIRL.

LOVE YOU"

Another example: I was speaking with a couple of my students at my desk recently; one is relatively new to our program, and the other has been with us for awhile. The 'new' one noticed a lesson plan for my Missouri Natural Science class and said;

"I want to be in that class next year."

I informed the student that it was a lot of work, but, it was one of my more popular classes.

"All of her classes are good," said the older student, "she's strict, but, her classes are always good, and she's fun but strict at the same time."

(O.K. I get it, I can be fairly strict).

"Hey, I'm sitting right here," I reminded them, pretending to be offended. More seriously I said, "I don't want to be that strict; but, you know why I have to be *so* strict on the class you're in."

"Yeah, I know. I get it, you have no choice," the student replied, " and I don't mind, it's still a good class."

Not all At-Risk students are looking for an argument. Most of them have enough of that in their lives. On the other hand, if you allow it to escalate, they won't back down either. Over the years, I can honestly say, the majority of my students just want a place where they feel like they belong. They want to know that you're not "out to get them." They want to know that you want them to succeed. That you respect them as human beings. They want to know you will see them as an individual and not judge them for the mistakes their family has made in the past (like I said before...it's a small town). I can't recall the number of students, over the years, that have told me they have had teachers that will judge them due to the behavior of an older sibling that has been in their classes. Or, at least, that was the way it felt to them. Right now I have at least three. They want you to be as fair as possible. They want you to keep your word. I firmly believe that most of these kids want to take a break from being the 'adult' in their lives and just want to feel secure, if for just a little while. I wish these same things for them, and I consistently tell them so.

I don't have a lot of studies or stats of my own to back up my methods. What I do have is over 20 years of trial and error. Over 20 years of laughing, crying, and learning. An accumulation of everything I have studied and read, tried, kept and rejected. Over twenty years of figuring out what works best for my students and me. Finding my new center.

---

Since I'm talking about rules, I need to clarify the different types of rules. There are the individual classroom rules that vary slightly from one teacher to the next, and there are the building rules. Our program had three main building rules in the beginning:

1. **No fighting-** whoever threw the first punch was automatically out of the program. No second chances.
2. **No drugs or alcohol**—same consequences as #1
3. **No leaving the building without permission**—same consequences as #'s 1 and 2.

I miss those rules. Years ago, someone decided that if we had rules of absolutes, there wouldn't be as many options to help the students; at least, that is what I was told when I questioned their removal. To this day I'm still not sure who's idea it was to dismantle the rules. I'm pretty sure it wasn't the teachers idea. Either way, the original rules are gone or so watered down they are not nearly as effective, and that is a pity.

I might have been okay with letting go of #3. At-Risk kids are notorious for being hotheads, or maybe that applies to most teenagers. A quick temper certainly could have been attributed to me at that age. It took a lot of time, work, and growing up for me to learn how to rein in my temper.

Sometimes they just need a little cool-off time so they will not be overcome with the temptation to break Rule #1. Not to mention that walking out the door without permission is relatively common in their home lives. I always thought that if a turn around the parking lot could help them gain their composure and do the right thing, then that would be a reasonably decent coping mechanism. Let's be honest; if a child is so angry, they are ready to walk-away they are probably not really in the mood to learn about *'plate tectonics'* or care what *Gregor Mendel* did with his peas. In time they learned to trust and respect us enough to come to one of us before taking off. They also learned to trust and respect us enough to return; but, more importantly, they learned to trust and respect themselves enough to come back.

Rule #2 was a bit harder to let go of, and if memory serves me I wasn't the only one that had a hard time letting go of that one. I reported a student that had come to my class high. The child was gone within the hour. Side-note; fortunately the student did get help and came back to visit with me from time to time. Somewhat contrite on the first visit, but, clear-eyed and coherent. Surprisingly, that first visit was to Thank me for turning him in. I just hope he is still clear-eyed and coherent.

At another time, I, along with my colleagues, repeatedly

reported that one of our girls was back on meth. She was called to the office, talked to, and it was reported back to us that she was okay. Her explanation for her behavior in the classrooms and hallways was due to not feeling well and a lack of sleep. Well, of course, she wasn't 'feeling or sleeping well' she was using again! A short time later, she was back in rehab. What happens when she gets out? She is back in our school and back in my classroom blaming me because I knew she was back on the meth and why didn't I turn her in to somebody? Some days it just doesn't pay to get out of bed. Events like that are the reason teachers occasionally take 'mental health' sick days.

Rule #1 is the one that should still be on the books for many reasons. As far as I'm concerned it should be on all the books; but, especially in an At-Risk school. First, it made the students feel safer. I have had many students tell me that at least if they did get hit by another student, they knew they wouldn't have to see that particular person in the halls, sit by them in class, the cafeteria, or accidentally meet them in the bathroom again. As I said before, the building is very small, and there was no way to avoid one another. One less stress factor in the lives of children that already had more than enough stress. Feeling less pressure and safer makes for a more focused and engaged student.

Second, I can't recall the number of times I had heard some of our 'bad boys' (and a few 'bad girls') proclaim to me, in front of a room full of students, they wanted to hit so-n-so. But didn't because: "I have a good thing going here. I'm going to graduate, and I didn't think I would. So, I'm not going to let (**insert name here**) mouthing cause me to mess it up and get kicked out. What do I care what he says?"

WoW! No fight.

The exact wording by each of the students may not have always been the same, but, the sentiment was. Within Rule #1 we had given the student a legitimate, perfectly understandable excuse ***not*** to take a swing. He/she was able to save face.

Saving face is of importance to all of us, but it is of paramount importance to an At-Risk student that has a reputation to uphold. So many of them feel as if they cannot show any weakness. He/she would then be praised by me and by the other teachers for being the bigger person...acting like the adult in the situation by doing what was right for him/her. Praise for not allowing themselves to be goaded into making a bad choice. In turn, this would usually get the other half of the quarrel equation to back-off. A chance to cool down and re-think that being the tough guy didn't always get you the respect and attention you were looking for, neither from the teachers or the other students. I call that a win for everyone.

Before this rule was watered down, we had had only one incident in our first six years. If memory serves me well, it occurred in our second year. The student that instigated the incident was not allowed on our campus again, and word spread rapidly among the teen population of our program, and the main campus. We enforced our rules; no second chances. We did not have another incident for approximately four years.

There is a maxim that I have frequently heard among teachers, "If it's not broke, don't fix it." We were not broken, but, I can not say the same now. Now I think we're a little fractured. My colleagues and I, still hold it together with a bit of super-glue as best we can. I have often had people to ask me, "Why do you stay there, and continue to work with 'those kids'? Why don't you try to transfer to the regular high school?" I always answer with a question of my own, "Where do you think 'those kids' come from?" The majority of 'those kids' are primarily pretty good kids; most of the time, simply getting them out of the crowds on the main campus can make a big difference in their behavior. Usually, they just need a little extra understanding.

There were those that argued the consequences for the no fighting rule was too draconian. That's when the consequence for fighting turned into OSS (out of school suspension, ten days) rather than automatic expulsion from our program. Since then, over the past twelve years, there have been several instances of one student physically harming or attempting to harm another student physically, but, no permanent expulsions from our program. I argue, draconian or not, it worked.

How many at-risk programs, or mainstream schools, can boast of only one physical altercation among its students in six years? One must remember, that when dealing with the at-risk student, one is dealing with a person that is the epitome of draconian views. For the at-risk student, actions are either right or wrong; there are no gray areas. If you give them an inch of wiggle room, they will go for three inches. They need cut and dried rules. They understand absolutes. An absolute rule tells them where they stand; exactly how far they can go before they have crossed-the-line of no return. Because, the at-risk student does not merely dance up to, or around, the line; they will charge the line.

# 6 Talk the talk...better, Walk the walk

This may not be a startling revelation to anyone else; but, I was a bit surprised. Did you know that regardless of the limited vocabulary of a teenager (and perhaps preteens as well) there is one word they all seem to know?

NO, not that one. It's the 'H' word.

**Hypocrite**

Never delude yourself into thinking that your students aren't paying attention to you. They may not be listening as attentively as you would like to the content of your lecture; but, they are paying attention to you personally. I have had students to notice and comment when I changed the color of my nail polish, if I wear something new, cut my hair, know the number of rings I wear. O.k., I have to admit, I do have quite a collection on my hands; but, you get the idea. This is boys and girls alike. They do not merely notice how you look, but, they notice how you act and speak. And, most importantly, they are paying particular attention to whether or not what you say correlates to your behavior. They watch you interacting with other students. They watch you interact with other teachers, the principal, visitors in the building. Just about the time, you think they aren't paying attention, is when you are at your most vulnerable.

Try this sometime, wherever you see two or more teachers gathered to have a quick word with one another...take notice of the students near them. They may have been in a huddle, that two seconds before was full of whispers and laughter; but, has now suddenly hushed. The same kid that didn't hear the instructions the first, second, or third time that day in class, is suddenly all ears if he/she observes teachers talking. Surprised by the 'he/she' reference? Don't let your preconceived notions fool you. In my experience, there is no difference between boys and girls when a little gossip is going around. Another anomaly is the student that normally enters the classroom doing what I call 'slamming and jamming.' You've seen them; they don't place their belongings on the desk or table— they slam them on the desk or table. They don't just walk into the room; they bounce into the room. They don't greet their buddies and friends already in the room with a simple "Hi, Hey or Hello" they're yelling their greeting. It's incredible but, that same boisterous student can slip in behind you quiet as a mouse to pick-up whatever juicy little tidbits they think they might hear.

I have seen students that are masters at covert ops. Hiding around corners, stepping between the door and the wall. And, when caught eavesdropping will say, "Oh I didn't want to be rude and interrupt." Uh-huh, sure. So if you're gonna 'talk the talk' you better 'walk the walk.' Never is that more true than with the At-Risk student. I know, I know, it should be true for all students and adults for that matter. But, the At-Risk student is watching and waiting for you to slip-up. Remember the story about my daughter and her losing respect for her teacher? The thing is she told *me* that story, but, she never said anything to the teacher. An At-Risk student is a complete opposite; they will call you on it. Sometimes very publicly. For instance, in front of a class, or they will tell other teachers of your hypocrisy, or announce it in the cafeteria or a crowded hallway.

By the way, this furtive behavior doesn't just happen in a school setting with students and teachers. Take notice of any child above the age of—let's say three—and start a whispered conversation with someone in the room or on the phone. Suddenly, the child that was bouncing off the walls becomes quiet and seemingly focused on a toy, the hem of their pants, their shoe, etc. Move into the next room or step outside while still in conversation and amazingly the child whose attention you couldn't get a few minutes ago is now following you.

*"An ounce of practice is worth more than tons of preaching."*
**— Mahatma Gandhi**

I am reminded of a story that was told by family friends. The parents had grounded their young daughter, for some reason that escapes me now, for a month. Long before the month was up the parents were going nuts. They had to stay home with her. She complained, she needed to be entertained, her friends called regularly and frequently to cheer her up (this was before cell phones) tying up the home phone. Not only had they grounded her for a month, but they had also unwittingly grounded themselves for a month in the process. They warned my parents if they ever had to ground me, to make sure it was something they could live with for the duration. After that, I think our friends decided that a week was plenty of time for their kids to learn a lesson.

So when you pick your 'talk' make sure it's something that you can and will 'walk.' Make sure it's something you can live with all day; every day. In other words, make sure you are willing to practice what you preach. If you call them on punctuality; then don't be late for class. If your focus is on the use of foul language; make sure you don't use it. If making fun/name calling of one another is something you will not tolerate from them; make sure you do not mock. To put it plainly don't expect your students to behave in more of an adult manner than you, yourself. Be the adult in the room.

I have had students to come to me and allude (or downright accuse) fellow faculty members both near and far (faculty from other buildings) of hypocrisy in some form. I hate to say it, but, the truth is, some of our little darlins' love to play one teacher against another. Sometimes there may be some validity to what they say, sometimes not; but, I have learned, the hard way, it's best not to engage.

I try to keep my response as neutral as possible with something like the following: "I can't control other people's conduct, I can only control my own. Do you hear me using inappropriate language? Am I late for class? Do you hear me seriously calling people names or making fun of them?" Oh by the way; don't ask questions like that unless you're sure the correct answer goes your way to prove your point. I also encourage the student to have a private conversation with the teacher about their complaint. However, as I pointed out previously, don't expect it to be a *private* conversation.

According to Albert Bandura, social-learning theorist and psychologist from the late 1970's: *"Behavior is learned from the environment through the process of observational learning."*

It's my opinion that we should model the behavior we want from our students. If we don't practice what we preach, then we can expect and need to be prepared for their ridicule. They will be quick to point out: (using their own vernacular), "You talk it, but you don't walk it." And, another chunk of their respect for authority bites the dust.

# 7 Prayer-in-School

This chapter will be concise. I will give you my thoughts on this subject and leave it there. First of all, never let anyone tell you there is no prayer in school. I believe I mentioned before, that I keep a running dialogue with God in my head. I wasn't being flippant. I was, and I am serious. Not a year has passed that I don't have one or more students tell me they are an atheist. Not a year has passed that I haven't had one or more students ask me to please pray for them if I believe in God. Not a day goes by that I'm not asking God to give me the words I need to reach my students, and I pray for His help to be what he needs me to be for my students.

There has been so much argument about whether or not to have prayer in schools. Trust me; if I'm at work, there is definitely prayer in at least one public school. My private prayers may not go far enough for some people who want prayer to be taught in our school systems and maybe too far for those that do not; but, no one is allowed to dictate what is in my mind. I'm at peace with it.

Please read the following for a more accurate and straightforward explanation:

> Matthew 6:5-6 King James Version (KJV)
>
> 5 And when thou prayest, thou shalt not be as the hypocrites are: for they love to pray standing in the synagogues and in the corners of the streets, that they may be seen of men. Verily I say unto you, They have their reward.
>
> 6 But thou, when thou prayest, enter into thy closet, and when thou hast shut thy door, pray to thy Father which is in secret; and thy Father which seeth in secret shall reward thee openly.

When talking religion, I refer to myself as a Jesus follower. I attempt to live my life as he has told us to live. I'm human, so, therefore, I don't always succeed. My personal belief in the manner that we are to pray, does not lend itself to public group prayer as dictated by the words of Jesus in Matthew. Therefore, I would not be comfortable attempting to force people to pray or to punish them if they do not. I am a biology teacher, not a theologian.

Truthfully, I believe in God, I believe in Jesus, and I believe in the power of prayer. If it were not for my belief, I don't think I would be capable of doing this job. However, I will do my praying in my closet.

# 8 Some of my Favorite Stories

Being an at-risk teacher is not all rules/regulations, frowns and formality, there are many good times too. One story that comes to mind concerns a young man that thought he would never survive in college classes.

First I need to explain that when we started this program, we started with the bare basics for each classroom. Tables, chairs, a teacher's desk, a couple of bookshelves, one computer in each room (for the teacher's use), a large storage cabinet, a file cabinet, a whiteboard and dry erase markers. We did not have any textbooks or resource materials in the beginning. We had to create our own lessons.

In my university classes, I was fascinated with genetics, and I had chosen to teach a modified Genetics class for the first semester, and Anatomy the second. I based this class for the entire semester on the introduction to my junior year genetics class (remember we only had 35 minutes a day per class). I wrote my own lectures and created my worksheets; some of them were hand-printed (longhand) and then run through the copy machine. I drilled them on the introductory vocabulary, and mechanics necessary for understanding the basics for genetics, introduced them to the Father of Genetics-Gregor Mendel. We created Punnett square problems until by the middle of the semester they were crossing up to four traits (this is a 64 square problem), and then we tackled the history of cloning: from peas to Dolly, the sheep. I did not tell my students their lessons were taken from my college textbook and my college class notes, when I was a junior; in fact, I kept the book hidden until we neared the end of the introduction. Then I pulled it out, showed it to them, and told them they had completed the work of the first few classes of a college-level genetics class. I made it quite clear to them that there was much more to the subject, but, they had successfully done work that I had seen some college classmates struggle to do and that they should take great pride in their success.

At the end of the class (in our very first semester) I noticed that one young man was dawdling a bit before following his buddies to their next class.

"Everything alright?" I asked as he beckoned me into the hallway for some privacy.

"Yeah, I just had a question," he said, in a somber tone of voice and he was quite interested in his shoes, he wasn't looking at me.

"You're in luck...it's early in the day, and I still have a few answers left in me," I quipped, trying to lighten the mood.

"Were you serious about that work being college level?" he asked.

"Yes. Like I said it's just the beginning, but, I pretty much taught you what I was taught in the first few weeks of my genetics class." I said. "What are you getting at?"

He made eye-contact then. What I saw was stunning; his eyes were filled with tears.

The mommy in me came to the forefront, "What's wrong, sweetie?"

"I didn't think I could ever do college work," he stated. "And it wasn't even that hard."

"You're sure that's what we were doing?" he asked again. "I thought I would be doing good to get my high school diploma.

I didn't think I could do college work. But, I did, I really did?" he asked once more.

From what I knew of this child's background I was reasonably sure this lack of confidence in his academic abilities had not come from home.

Looking him in the eyes, I said, "You can do it, you did do it, and if it's what you want, you will do it."

Fast forward a couple of years: that student went on to the college of his choice (thanks to a very nice score on the ACT) and later joined the military.

Funny, but, I can remember that day as if it were last week. I was once asked by a student, years later, in the middle of a genetics class as I was reviewing vocabulary in preparation for a worksheet they were about to be given: "Why is this even a class?" Hmmmm, Genetics as a science class…not a new concept. Clearly, he didn't care for the subject matter. This is what I meant before about the students that come to us thinking it's just an alternative school, so I don't have to do anything...I don't have to put in any work. His stay with us was quite short.

So, whenever, I feel like I'm banging my head against a wall; I stop, I take a deep breath, I dust off the old memory of the young man with tears in his eyes and remember— this is why I teach. This is why I teach at-risk.

---

Have you ever had a favorite comedian that really tickled your funny-bone just by looking at them or hearing them laugh? Eddie Murphy comes to mind. I have heard people say that just hearing him laugh made them laugh. The comedian Tim Conway had that effect on my dad. All Mr. Conway had to do was walk on-stage, and my dad would start laughing. He simply couldn't help himself.

I had a student that affected me like that. In our early years, we had this one student that was just a great kid; all of the teachers loved him, and he was well-liked by his peers. He had a good heart, sweet, smart enough, and a class clown. Now I had met those before but, was not usually that amused by them. This kid was different. He knew how to laugh at himself without self-flagellation and knew how to make others laugh. I could very well understand the reason he would be disruptive in a mainstream classroom; but, here, well...he was still disruptive, and I couldn't do a darn thing about it. Because he was sweet and smart, and he had a good heart. His joking was never hurtful and very witty. One day I had to keep redirecting him to get him to finish an assignment.

"Maybe I don't want to do it," he said giving me a side-way smile; lacking any rancor.

I smiled back, "You don't have to want to...you just have to do it."

I left him for a bit to assist another student, when I turned back to him he was nearly finished,

"I thought you didn't want to, and you're nearly done. Good work too, from what I can see," I said, looking over his shoulder.

He then turned, looked up at me with a deadpan expression and very quietly said, "My parents."

"What?" I was confused.

Continuing with the same quiet (unusual for him) tone, and an incredibly forlorn expression, he said, "My parents and their damn work ethic. I couldn't stop myself from finishing."

I knew I was supposed to call him down for using inappropriate language to the teacher in the classroom, but, he was my Tim Conway...instead, I started laughing. This is what always happened when I would try to correct him. I was useless with this kid as a disciplinarian. All he had to do was look at me, and I was a mess. If we were in a whole school group activity and I saw him doing something he shouldn't, I would have to get one of the other teachers to correct him. Not that they were much better off than I, when dealing with this young man, but, they could usually at least keep a straight face while calling him down. To my knowledge, he grew up to be a very responsible husband, father, and businessman. I hope his kids are as mischievous as he was. I miss Tim Conway.

---

Cell phones! When our daughter started driving I thought they were a godsend; we bought a mobile bag phone the day she got her drivers permit. For those of you that are too young to remember bag phones they were quite simply a phone, nothing more, you could make calls and receive calls. There was nothing inconspicuous about these phones, they were contained in a small bag, with a strap to carry on your shoulder. The only other option was 'the brick' hand-held phone. No bag, and the brick had the additional feature of doubling as a small dumbbell. The brick weighed about 2 pounds, had about 30 minutes of talk-time before needing to be recharged, and a rather limited range; but, the bag phones had the longest range and a little longer on the charge. Our daughter was now on the road...sold!

Between the advent of the bag/brick phones and the current smart-phones was the flip-phone. Along with being smaller and lighter the user of a flip phone would be greeted by its glowing green or blue light upon opening, and they had the capability of texting. The popularity and availability of the flip-phones were immediate. They were becoming common enough among our students to warrant a verbal warning to put them away at the beginning of each class.

One afternoon I had decided to show an educational video to accompany the lesson plan, and I reminded those of my students that had them to put away their phones as I made my way to the light switch. Upon turning to face the class, after turning off the lights, I noticed that one young woman still had her phone out. I told her to put the phone on my desk. She informed me, with a bit of indignation, that she didn't have her phone out. "Really," I asked? The other students in the room turned to look at her and burst into laughter. I have to admit I really wanted to laugh too. There she sat, in all of her defiance's, bathed in a lovely blue light that emanated from the open phone on her lap. The entire corner of the room was alight from the phone, and she was glowing like an alien from an old sci-fi movie.

Cell phones are the bane of a teachers workday. The majority of my discipline problems are connected to the use of a cell phone in some capacity. Academic dishonesty and focus on the phone rather than the lesson are among some of the problems. But, maybe the worst grievance I have is when I greet a perfectly happy, smiling student at my door who turns into a crying mess within seconds. The reason? Someone has sent a text or posted something hurtful concerning the student. Or, that happy student becomes so angry they are beginning to lose control; because someone posted something hateful or false or betrayed a secret about the student. When I think of all the problems that can be attributed to the use of cell phones and social media within the school systems, I long for the days of the bag/brick phones. Make a call—receive a call, nothing more.

# 9 Tragedies and Triumphs

During my years of at-risk teaching, I have laughed until I cried and, for various reasons, I have cried until I learned to laugh again. The hardest thing I have had to face...that every teacher has had to face; is the death of a student. Regardless, of whatever evil took them away from this earth, the reality is the same. No more smiles, frowns, high fives, hugs, laughter, teasing, singing, or arguments from this person again; and all I know is that I want them back. For the sake of my other students, I save the majority of my tears for later. I mourn for what could have been.

Having a student to choose to fail is its own kind of tragedy. Fortunately, it doesn't have to be permanent; that is entirely up to the individual. I have had Seniors drop-out of school two weeks before graduation. Two weeks!! Why would a person do that? The only explanation I have ever come up with is a fear of succeeding, a fear that peoples' expectations would be higher once they had graduated? I don't have an answer, but, I have seen self-sabotage by more than one student. Thankfully, it's not the norm, but it does happen.

I have had students to tell me, since the beginning of my teaching career, they wouldn't work for a teacher because they didn't like him/her. Not only, students, but parents as well. Choosing not to work for a teacher is a pretty quick way to fail that teacher's class.

Case in point: I'm at one of our annual parent/teacher meetings, and I have the parents of a 'new to us' student in my room. I have introduced myself, asked who their student is and I pulled the work out for their child. I give them a moment to look over the work, and they keep shooting glances at each other and back to me.

Not understanding, precisely what is transpiring between the two, I say, "The grades are good, and as long as *Johnny* continues with this quality of work he should be successful in my class."

The parents who are now scrutinizing me rather closely give me a big smile and say; "*Johnny* must really like you, because, he won't work for you unless he likes you."

Really? I have never understood that one; and I have had that conversation more times than I care to think about. It is an unrealistic attitude for parents or teachers to indulge for any future endeavors of the child. I refuse to accept this as an excuse. When this occurs, the student has now earned the Ms. Donna lecture on that big bad world out there:

"You know, I have already passed this class, it's your turn now. You aren't hurting me (or whatever teacher they are complaining about), you are hurting yourself. There is a very real chance that someday you will have a boss that you don't like. There is a very real chance you will have to work alongside people you don't like. Now, you can stop working; which will get you fired or you can quit your job; but, you're the one that will be without a paycheck, not them. You can refuse to do your lessons and fail your class; but, you're the one that will be without a diploma, not me/him/or her. If a diploma isn't your end goal; then why are you here? Don't answer me now, just think about it."

Sometimes the lecture will reach them; not that they will admit to it at the time. There will still be some blustering, and that's alright. Remember, they have to save face. So I give them space to think about it. It will need to appear as if they had decided on their own, to make a change in their work habits, and it had nothing to do with what I have said to them. I let them tell themselves and anyone that will listen it was all their decision; because, the truth is, it is their decision and always was. I have had occasion to know that my little lecture has had some influence over a few kids, but, I don't bring it up again. If they're working; then I got what I wanted. I don't need to flaunt it.

But, I have to be prepared, sometimes it doesn't work. Letting go and letting a kid fail is one of the hardest things I have to do occasionally. Fortunately, I can usually needle, pester, cajole, sit beside them, or stand over them, until they concede and do the work. I secretly, figure they do it so that they can get away from me. But, I have met some students that are more stubborn than I am and appear to be hellbent on failing. And there comes a time when they have to want their success at least a little bit. Not to mention I do have other students that want and need help in finding their success. When it becomes glaringly apparent (yes, glaringly, didn't I mention before that I'm tenacious?) that I want their success more then they want it for themselves, I back off. I become a monitor more or less to those students. I hand out their assignments, I give the instructions, if they have lesson based questions I answer and I just let them sit as long as they are not disturbing anyone else. If and when they're ready to try again, I will be right by their side if needed and I will be their biggest cheerleader; but, they have to give me something to work with, they have to want it, too.

Apparently, and I'm speaking from my personal, professional experiences and from reading every piece of research I could get my hands on; this attitude of "I only work for those I like," is VERY common among At-Risk students. It is that attitude that makes the 'relationship and rapport' building so very vital with At-Risk kids.

Trust, honesty and sincerity, plain speaking without demeaning, genuine compassion and respect, empathy without overwhelming sympathy, listening without judgment; these are the primary elements needed to create a world of affability between you and your At-Risk students. It's a lot of work and if the sincerity isn't genuine on your behalf, they will know. But, if you can build that bridge, the reward on the other side will continue into their lives and yours.

You know a bridge has been built when you are out shopping, and you suddenly find yourself in a big bear hug, or someone is calling your name from across the store. Past students, anywhere from a year ago to 18 years ago, are introducing you to their companions, and many times are proudly proclaiming this was my teacher. A somewhat humbling experience, but one that is welcome.

You know that the bridge has been built when they keep coming back to visit after they have graduated. These visits have become a new normal for me. At first I always felt surprise when I would open my door to a student from five years ago or five weeks. I had no experience with students going back to visit their high school teachers. Not that I didn't have perfectly wonderful teachers but, I didn't have the kind of relationship with them as these students have with me and my colleagues. I guess the difference is that I didn't need to. My cheerleaders were at home. I had support at home. Here, hardly a week goes by without a visit from a former student. There is nothing unusual in our having anywhere from one to five former students to visit in a period of one week. I think the most, former students, I have seen in one day is six.

They bring their babies and their toddlers to us to show them off; they want to tell us about their jobs, their wives or husbands, or their latest loves. They want to tell us about their lives, mostly, they want to know we are still interested in their lives, they want to know we still care. In years past we have had former students come to us after school for a little extra tutoring with their college classes, and we happily oblige. When they come back, and we see our past students wearing military uniforms, nursing smocks, smelling of oil-grease-or welding smoke on their way to work or just getting off a shift; just to know they are gainfully employed, furthering their educations or sometimes both; these are the things that I and my colleagues work for everyday. After all, isn't that our ultimate goal as teachers? To see these young people living a good productive life. Young people that had been written off by some in conventional society. Maybe, just maybe, we contributed a little bit to the good things in the lives of these past students. As teachers, their triumphs are our triumphs. This is the reason I teach At-Risk.

# 10 Myths About the Alternative School and the At-Risk Student

"Oh, that's the school for the bad kids." "That's the school for pregnant teenagers." "That's where the stupid kids go." "That's not a real school, they don't have to do anything there." I have heard all that and much worse to describe our school and our student population. These are the primary myths that surround the at-risk youth and an alternative school.

So I have decided to discuss them one at a time. And, by discuss I mean I will state my viewpoint, as I have from the beginning of this book, on each item.

**Myth 1:**
*"That's the school for pregnant teenagers."*

My viewpoint on this myth is short and quite simple. Yes, we have had some students that have been pregnant and/or young men who are about to be fathers. Doesn't every high school?

No, not every pregnant teen in our district is sent to our school. But, even if they were, so what? An education and a diploma offers options, opportunities, and opens doors does it not? So rather than a statement I have a question for those skeptics that want to label our program as a "School for Wayward Mothers": Whom among our teen population needs an education more than a youth about to become a parent?

**Myth 2:**

*"Oh, that's the school for the bad kids."*

O.k. I'll give you that the majority of alternative school programs are filled with students that are considered to be behavioral problems. Wasn't I afraid of that in the beginning? However, our educational program really is different, or it was. It seems of late, more and more of our students most assuredly have some behavioral issues. Issues that my colleagues and I are ill-equipped to handle and rightfully so. Our program was never meant to serve genuinely behavioral students.

In my experiences with students that exhibit behavioral issues I have noticed certain across- the-board traits; certain consistencies. First, as a general rule, they are very bright individuals and they will attempt to be quite manipulative. Sometimes they are successful. Secondly, they look at themselves as an adult, your equal. They also want you to see them as your equal; intellectually and authoritatively. By the way, I always tell my kids that if you have to say to me or remind me that you're an adult, chances are you're not. Third, these are the kids that will never back down as long as they have an audience of their peers.

Ready for a little amateur psychoanalysis into the psyche of the behavioral student? Be warned! I will be basing this layman's theory on the handful of behavioral students that I have dealt with over the years. Here goes.

Because they are very bright they don't feel they fit in with people their own age and never have; in turn, they can become very socially awkward. If they are true to their nature and act too 'brainy' in front of their peers they will be labeled as a suck-up, a teacher's pet or whatever defamatory slang is currently popular with grade school and middle school aged children that equates to the golden-oldie: a nerd. They cannot seem to reconcile their intelligence level with the social nuances of their age group.

Have you ever heard someone say, "I don't understand! *Joey* is normally such a bright kid." They are referring to academically bright.

"Why would he pull a stunt like that?" They are referring to the lack of *common sense* exhibited by *Joey*. Some random act of stupidity that could have gotten *Joey* hurt. It could mean that because Joey is so smart he must experiment or Joey is a smart kid trying to fit-in by being the daredevil. If it's the latter, these kids from grade school to high school just can't seem to find their niche. So how do they get the attention of their peers they so desperately crave?

Become the "bad boy" of course. This behavior will garner attention, a form of acceptance; perhaps, on some level a little admiration from their peers by acting out, and taking on any representative of authority. Being the 'daredevil' as it were. These are the kids who will escalate from simple non-compliance to screaming profanities before slamming out of the room in 60 seconds or less.

I have learned, from my experiences, if I can take away their audience and work with them one-on-one they can be, (not always), a completely different kid. As a teacher I can understand, and appreciate their aptitude. Encourage them to "WOW" me with their intelligence and their inquisitiveness. Heap on the praise they desire and rarely, if ever, receive from people their own age. They can hold a conversation on a higher more mature level and be understood, rather than when they are conversing with their counterparts. They're counterparts can become uncomfortable and instead of engaging them in conversation find a reason to leave. This can cause the behavioral student to become contentious. But, without anyone watching they have no need to take on a belligerent attitude. They can drop the "bad boy" facade and be the student that has the capability of advancing fairly rapidly through their academics. Of course, having been employed as a classroom teacher rather than a private tutor the opportunities to work with them in the setting I described are rare. These individuals that are consistently in trouble are the reason I think there should be an alternative to the alternative school. A program that will fast track them through their high school years. An academically self-contained program that is saved for a select few; for the behavioral, but bright young person. Perhaps held after regular school hours, because let's be honest here, these young people are never going to fit in with their own age group. They hit age 16 at the age of 10. They need to move on. They are usually a detriment in a classroom. A detriment to those children that are more academically challenged and/or have their own emotional life issues. I think of these children as the 'emotional barometer' in the room. The kids that are always standing on the precipice. These are the ones that can hold it together as long as nothing pushes at them too hard. These are the kids that live on the edge of emotional collapse that can result in a full-blown outburst with the slightest nudge at any given time. These are the children that our program was initially designed for, and the ones that I am accustomed to working with on a daily basis. But, throw-in a behavioral student (whom we were not designed for) that is feeling neglected and suddenly the steady barometer in the room is falling. Lightning flashes, thunder rolls, and no one cares about the dominant versus recessive alleles anymore and there goes my genetics class. Learning comes to a screeching halt. Which is why I believe consistently behavioral students are in a class of their own and they need a class of their own.

### Myth 3

*"That's where the stupid kids go."*

This is the one that hurts the most, and in my opinion, does the most harm to my students. Most of the students we cater to are woefully under-educated; not incapable of learning as the word 'stupid' would imply. "Why are they under-educated?" We may as well ask, "How many stars are in the sky?" The answers to both questions are too varied and too numerous to nail down into one definitive answer. But, some of the more common reasons I have observed for a student to be under-educated are as follows: too many days in ISS (in-school-suspension) rather than in the classroom, illnesses, a less than desirable home life, their learning rate is less than expected or they need more time given to complete an assignment, etc. Regardless of the reason, the reality is that I have a job to do. Teach. However, the first thing I have to battle is to get my students to overcome the myth that they are in my classroom because they are stupid. More times than I can count I have had students to tell me, "Yeah but you're smarter that I am. You're the teacher."

My reply? "You don't know that. You might be a lot smarter than I am." Jaws will drop and a hush will fall over the room. So I continue, "Obviously, I have lived longer than you so I have had more life experiences. For you, certain past events are nothing more than dry historical facts, names, dates, and places. But, for me, they are memories. I saw a man walk on the moon in real time. I also know that I have a lot more education than you currently have. But, I don't know, and you don't know if I'm smarter than you, only time will tell." I have had students to tell me they're surprised that since I'm a teacher that I would admit that. The truth is I have had several students that I'm pretty sure has a higher I.Q. than I. The fact is that my most of students are perfectly capable of learning; we just have to start back at the basics. And, with that I will discuss Myth 4.

### Myth 4

*"That's not a real school, they don't have to do anything there."*

I mentioned this one before. It seems that everyone buys into this one, including some of our students...in the beginning.

Most of our students are shocked that they have note-taking, handouts and worksheets, research, and projects to do on a daily basis with a test thrown in for good measure every now and again. In my classes, each class, they have a little something extra to do; build their own textbook (I call them portfolios). I rarely use textbooks and for the classes that I have created there isn't a textbook; therefore, it is necessary for them to make their own textbook for reference. They start with a 2 or 3 inch 3 ring-binder, page protectors, a pre-printed Table-of-Contents page and colored card- stock. They must create a cover for their textbook. They must keep, organize, and number all notes, handouts, and graded worksheets and write it all down on their Table of Contents page in their binders just like a textbook. If I give them a 3-page handout with a 2-page worksheet that equals five pages, front to back, in the book. This is a big part of their grade. The book becomes their property upon completion of the course. Parents love them, and my students can't believe the amount of work they have done at the end of the course. I have had former students to tell me they still have their books and still look at them occasionally or their children will look through them; particularly, the Missouri Natural Science book.

Surprisingly, I have had a few of my students to tell me they like making the book and they wished all the teachers would do it in their classes. They claimed they had never been so organized before. It may be fanciful wishing on my part; but, I think they like the idea of having something tangible as proof of their commitment to graduate. A way to say, "Hey, look at what I did!" Many of them are in awe of themselves that they have done so much. In a year-long class, they will have, approximately, 100 to 120 pages front-to-back of handouts, their research, and worksheets. Its also handy at Parent/Teacher meetings to be able to pull this out and show them what their child is or in some cases is not doing. You see I grade every paper I give them. Nothing made me angrier as when I was a student, and the teacher would decide, after I would work my butt off, to not take a grade on a paper. Besides I have found that the more points possible, the better chance my students will have at passing my classes. The school supply's the materials, and yes, it can be somewhat pricey. My budget goes to the binders and page covers; so, I buy the majority of my desk supplies: pens, pencil, paper clips, markers, etc. There have been many times when portfolio supplies run low, and I purchased them myself, but, on the other hand, I don't spend much on textbooks. I haven't had too many complaints.

# 11 How to Succeed in My Classroom

## My expectations:

- I expect for you to show respect to yourself, to your peers, and to me. Derogatory language and/or actions will not be tolerated.
- I expect you to enter my room in a reasonable manner, pick-up your portfolios, pencil or pen and to **put your phones away.** Backpacks are to be placed in a cubby at the back of the room and retrieved at the end of the block…do not leave them in my room.
- I expect for you to ask me questions when you don't understand the material being taught.
- I expect for you to be in attendance and to have your full attention during my class.

## Grading:

- 50% of your grades will be calculated from seat work and daily grades and 50% from your text portfolio.
  — Seat-work examples: worksheets, projects, research, etc.

- Daily grades: 10 points per day is possible (**there is no make-up work for these points).**

  **First,** in order to earn the 10 points, you must be in attendance and attentive (awake) in my classroom.

  — (ISS, OSS, all absences or being removed from my class for behavior will receive 0 points for each day outside of my classroom).

  **Second,** doing the work that has been assigned.

  — Examples: taking lecture notes, doing the seat work, participating in (or at least listening to) classroom discussions, updating portfolios, etc.
- Cell phones are not to be used in my classroom unless you have my permission individually.

## Exceptions to the rules:

- Daily grades will be suspended in cases of severe, documented illnesses/hospitalizations, funeral leave, counselor meetings.
- Cell phones: I understand that occasionally you might be expecting an urgent call (i.e., Parent/guardian, work-related, doctors office); first you need to tell me before class starts, then if/when comes through take your phone to the hallway to ensure your privacy and to limit classroom disruption.

Sign and Date: Your signature indicates that you understand my rules and expectations.

The preceding are my rules and expectations that I spoke of previously. I pass out a copy of my rules to my students every semester. I read them and explain as I go, even with the students that have heard it and signed before. I think a little reminder is a good thing.

The time spent in explaining my rules and expectations is

crucial. Not only does it inform my students about how I run my classroom; it also begins to lay the foundation for my relationship with my new students. This time, is also, my opportunity to let a little of my personality show through; while allowing me to gauge their reaction to me. I'm a big believer in reading body language.

To start: after reading the first expectation, this is when I talk about my room as being "my house." They are my guests, and I want them to feel welcome and comfortable while showing respect for my house, the other guests, and for me. I will point to a small sign on my desk that says: Be Nice or Leave –Thank You. Generally, this will garner a few giggles right-up to the moment I say, "I'm not kidding. Either, be nice, or you can visit the man down the hall. It is your choice." I also tell them, "I'm an old flower-child, so don't screw with my serenity." This will usually get some chuckles, mine included. I, sometimes, use this time to say, "Do not tell one another to shut-up while in my room. You can, however, tell someone to, *"Please refrain from speaking in my direction."* This directive will usually be the cause of more than a few bewildered expressions; because, students that have had my classes before will say it with me, in unison. Fun! I have learned that if students are yelling at each other to 'shut-up', a little laughter can go a long way toward defusing a tense situation. I can remember a college instructor say that teachers were at one time told not to smile until December. I think it's alright to laugh with my students and to enjoy being with them as long as I make my boundaries clear.

The next expectation, "…enter my room in a reasonable manner…." It's at this time I inform them not to come, "slamming and jamming into my room." This is where I will remind them that my room is not their locker, so they need to pick-up their things when they leave.

The third is one that I spend quite a bit of time explaining, "…ask me questions when you don't understand…." While it seems self-explanatory to me, it is one of the hardest things to get my students to follow. I try hard to inject a bit of humor into my lecture:

"Guess what? I get paid to answer your questions. Please let me know if you don't understand. If you are not 'getting it' then I'm not explaining it right for the way you learn. Besides, sometimes I have a funky way of saying things." This is when I will also tell them; they are not allowed to comment or complain if another student needs to have a concept explained more than once. If I have the patience to explain it numerous times, then, they will have to find the patience to listen numerous times. "I also create the majority of the worksheets you will be expected to do in all of my classes. I'm the person that wrote the worksheet, and I'm the one that has the red pen. So, please ask me, not the person next to you. If you can't find an answer, let me know. I will not give you the answer, but I will tell you where to find it."

There have been times that I have had children to say to me that they feel stupid for asking for help. I tell them that; "... the only stupid question is the one you don't ask. If you don't know, then, you don't know. So ask, I will tell you or we'll find the answer, and then you will know. There is no shame in not knowing something. The shame is when you're too stubborn to ask for help." It takes some time to get them to trust me. To believe, that I will not get cranky with them for asking for explanations or assistance.

As I said previously, cell phones are the bane of my day, probably, of every teachers day. I do inform my students that I do not owe them time to use their cell phones. In my classroom, it is an earned privilege. If they are caught with it without my permission, they are required to hand it over. It is put in my desk until the end of the day. If they balk at giving it up, they are written up and will be visiting the administrator for insubordination. Yet, even after having gone through all of my rules, I have taken phones on the first day of a semester. Like I said before, there will always be one student that will challenge, and test the waters. Now is the time to start building the trust. I am bound to keep my word.

To prove to my students that I'm not out to get them, and that I do try to be fair; I do have two exceptions:

Daily points: "If you have been ordered by a doctor to stay out of school I will not hold that against you, nor, will I hold it against you if your parent, grandparent, or sibling is hospitalized. This is beyond your control. I also believe it is shameful to hold funeral leave against a student or an adult. If a person has lost someone they love they have enough to deal with already."

Cell phones: "Talk to me, I can be reasonable."

I will not pretend to have all the answers, nor, will I try to tell you that my 'rules and expectations' eliminate all of my classroom problems. In order to achieve any success by using this document, I have to continually remind them at the beginning of class, "Put your phones away ."

# 12 You know you're a little off center when...

Going off-center is a gradual state-of-being. Or, at least it was for me. I wasn't aware that I had drifted off to the side. I was so focused on my 'kids,' that it wasn't until I would get into a conversation with adults that I became aware of a change in me.

I think the first thing I noticed was my lack of patience with adults. I'm reminded of a story about my daughter when she was in kindergarten. While at home one day, she was in a particularly difficult mood and I was at my wits-end. I turned and asked her the question that all parents have probably asked their little ones; "Do you act like this at school?"

With a shocked look on her little, fussy face, as if she couldn't believe I could entertain such a thought, she responded with a resounding "NO!"

"Well, then why do you act like this at home?" I asked, trying to get her to see reason.

She quieted and pondered my question for a moment. Very calmly and quite seriously, she said: " Because mommy, I used all my goodness at school."

Out of the mouths of babes: a person just can't be good all of the time, and I just can't be patient all of the time. I generally use up my daily quota of patience in my classroom. I have precious little patience left for an adult who is behaving in a manner that would earn one of my students a reprimand.

The next thing I noticed was the odd looks I would receive from adults. For instance, teachers in the mainstream, at district meetings, or seminars; and of course the people who knew me before the drifting occurred. Whenever teachers get together the conversation usually turns to their students at some point. Time is spent regaling one another with stories about student behaviors or circumstances surrounding their students they consider to be alarming or extraordinary. As with any storyteller, a teacher will look to their audience for signs of validation for their thoughts, feelings, and opinions about the story they have just told. I began to notice that some people would seem a bit taken aback when my reaction would be a mere shrug of my shoulders.

It's not that I don't take notice of what is occurring around me, but there are certain things that no longer register on my radar. Things like Easter egg hair color, or cat's eye contacts, or multiple piercings or a plethora of tattoos are not the types of things that I get worked up about anymore. I was a teenager in the 1970's. A time when teens were trying to 'find themselves.' We dressed differently, wore our hair differently, we were more outspoken than the previous generations (at least that's what the previous generations told us on a fairly regular basis). Teens are still seeking to find themselves, probably always have and probably always will.

Did I notice the first time a kid walked-in with blue hair? Sure I did. I probably had something to say about it to my colleagues at the time. But, did it really matter? No. Still the same child with the same smile, the same weaknesses, the same strengths…the same. Except now the student was peeking at me through a curtain of blue.

Now, I will admit to having a private chuckle upon entering our cafeteria one day. As I perused the group before me, it was quite evident that the fad of dying one's hair unusual colors had picked-up among our student population. As I surveyed the room, noting the various brilliant hair colors, it occurred to me that I could have walked in on the extras from a *Star Trek* taping, as they were breaking for lunch. But, they were not actors, nor were they, aliens, they were my students; trying to 'find themselves.'

It's funny how, as a teen, we try so hard to find our individuality, only to wake up one day to realize that the more we try to be different the more we look and act like everyone else our age. Perhaps that is the day we actually start down the road of self-discovery.

My next indicator was the day I realized that some of the more unusual stories concerning the lives of some of our students, that had shocked me in my early years, were no longer shocking. For instance, several years ago a student's parent had been released from prison and came home with their prison lover in tow. When told of this event as an excuse for the student's inappropriate behavior at school, my first reaction was, " So? That's no excuse."

As I heard the words coming out of my mouth, I knew I was probably off-kilter. So why, you might ask, was that my response? Because I had heard this tale before. An earlier time, different student, different reactions… same basic story. However, I was still startled by my initial response in the moment. What was I thinking? Of course this would be devastating for anyone, and more so for a teenager. However, the initial shock value just wasn't there. I knew I had some deep reflecting ahead of me. So I had to ask myself; was I becoming that jaded? That cynical? Or, was I just that worn out? Burnout seems to be the current catchphrase for what I appeared to be exhibiting.

Their life events are still just as heart rendering, but at some point, I began to realize it's not something I hadn't heard before with specific variances. I found myself wondering, have things always been this bad or are they getting worse? Was child molestation always this prevalent in our society? Child neglect? Child abuse? It seems like I can't watch a newscast or read a newspaper without coming across some atrocity involving a child. So, does that mean these things are occurring more frequently? Was it always there on this scale? Or, are we just getting better at reporting abuse; therefore we hear about it more frequently? Perhaps, the answer is a combination of both.

Whereas in the past, as a society, we had buried the ugliness; we are now encouraging our young people to stop living the life of a victim. To come forward and shine a light on that which has always existed.

All these questions with no clear answers. Was I in burnout phase? I still cared about my students; and I still cared about their education. I always wanted the best for them; I still enjoyed working with them. I finally, came to a conclusion. That self-preservation is a better phrase than burnout to describe me. A veteran teacher told me early in my career that I internalized too much of my students' problems, and the vet was worried I would get hurt. Perhaps that teacher was right. I've always tried to put myself in the shoes of another. I try to imagine how I would feel if 'that' happened to me… good or bad. But, now I was building walls to keep the hurt away. I tell myself that it's for the best that I'm not so easily shocked anymore. Whereas I might have been near hysteria and wringing my hands years ago, I can now think, and react with more surety, and more appropriately. I know who to contact now, and know the context for which I need to frame a report… if a report is needed. That's what I tell myself, but, I'm not sure I believe me. I began to worry that I had gone too far off-center.

So where did I go from this epiphany to pull myself back? Back to the basics. Back to what I know works when teaching at-risk. Celebrating the victories of the small battles; such as, finally getting that one student to understand a concept, to finish a project, to take some pride in doing a more than passable job on an assignment. Of finally, knowing when to use 'an' instead of 'a' — saw instead of seen, that a light year is a measurement of distance, not time. I could go on, but, I'm sure you get my drift. These are small battles. I have decided that if I can win enough small battles, maybe I can win the war. Or, if not the war, I can at the very least, advance my cause. Accepting the fact that I can't fix their lives is the first step to my self-preservation. However, there are things that I can do. I can listen without judgment. I can give my students a safe academic environment to explore. I can let them make mistakes and not belittle or ridicule them when those mistakes occur. Instead, I can help them to rectify the mistake and consistently make a point of letting them know: "It's o.k., we all make mistakes."

I will never go back to the days of my post-teacher center, but, I will move forward to a new center with a bit more understanding of the human condition. And, now perhaps you can better understand why hair color, tattoos, and piercings no longer warrant even a raised eyebrow from me.

By the way, I'm not a fan of the yellow or green hair; but, truthfully, I really love the color combination of a brilliant blue and black. Actually, I own a couple of outfits with that color combo. I don't want it on *my* head, but, I can admire it on someone else.

# 13 Philosophy of Teaching

Donna Pfannenstiel

My philosophy of teaching is founded
in Idealism. I believe that my
classroom should be a safe place for students to learn not only the
subject matter but, practical skills and
social graces to be applied to
the adult world. I believe it is imperative
that we as teachers hold our
students accountable (academically and
behaviorally), to teach and practice
(model) tolerance in an atmosphere
reflecting reality. I believe students
should be looked upon as individuals with
individual needs and talents.
I believe it is my responsibility to create an
atmosphere within the classroom
that encourages students to safely explore and gain a sense of self.
I believe teaching needs to be a constant
learning experience for the teacher: of
subject matter, method, and human nature.
In teaching, one should always
look to the future after reviewing,

reflecting and scrutinizing the past.
**Do what you have to do...So that**
**You can do what you want to do**

I wrote my philosophy of teaching as an assignment while I was simultaneously attending the university and teaching under a provisional. I was a novice when I wrote my theory of what my classroom should be and I had so much to learn. Oh boy, have I learned. I have had so many unique experiences since then. I have learned so much from my colleagues and others who have come before me that are willing to share their experiences. I am a veteran now, and the philosophy that was written by the novice so many years ago still rings true for me today. I always keep it posted in my classroom.

Not only do I keep it posted, but, I reread it from time-to-time to remind myself of my core values as a teacher; not only as a teacher but as a citizen of the human race. I don't want to lose sight of the fact that my students are human beings deserving of the respect due to all humans.

I recall a conversation I had, years ago, with an employee of the district, that kept referring to the "people" and the "students" almost as if they were different entities. The statement was something along the lines of; "...the people wanted that, and the students did, too." People? Students? Why the contrast between the two? As the conversation continued so did the differentiation of entities. It may be a small distinction, but, I found it a little unsettling and perhaps a little telling of how this person viewed young people. It was the same feeling then that I get today when I see those commercials that have a disclaimer that says, "These are real people, not actors." Well unless artificial intelligence is far more advanced than we know; actors are real people. How about: "These are real customers, not paid actors." How about: "The people wanted that, young and old." I honestly, don't believe the person meant it as an intentional snub, but perhaps it belied an unconscious belief; as if, due to their age 'students' are something "other than." Not old enough to be considered a person of any consequence just yet. Or, perhaps my imagination coupled with my *near* Psych Degree was in overdrive. Yes, I was six hours short of earning dual degrees, Biology, and Psychology. But I didn't want to wait to graduate ...*sigh*.

Another part of my philosophy that I still hold close to my heart is: "...create an atmosphere within the classroom that encourages students to safely explore and gain a sense of self." Our young people need a place to bounce ideas and thoughts, off of someone that will engage them to find either the truth or fallacy of the things that goes on in their minds. They need a secure spot to stretch their thoughts, ask questions, and work things out, whether it is about themselves or an academic concept. They need a place free of mockery or immediate dismissal of their thoughts due to their age. I try to give them that place within the walls of my classroom.

I know that I always want to see my students as individuals, with individual needs and talents. However, some days it's hard not to lump them all together. Some days I want to throw my hands up and say, "Ugh, teenagers!" When that feeling becomes overwhelming, I try to re-focus on just one child and think of something good about him or her. I will move on to another if I'm still feeling frustrated. There have been times that I have had to continue with that little exercise until the last bell of the day. Then tomorrow I start anew. I want never to forget they are people in their own right; with opinions and thoughts all their own.

The last two lines of my philosophy are essential to me. I don't ever want to be so full-of-myself that I lose sight of my belief that as long as there is breath in my body, I will still have something to learn. As I try to keep my ideas in the forefront, I will also continue to look to the future while reflecting and scrutinizing the past. I want to hold to my values with an eye to what has occurred when dealing with my students; the things that were successful and the things that were not. I want to keep an open mind and keep learning.

# 14 "What are we doing today?"

"What are we doing today?" Good question! Now, let's hope I have a good answer. As I mentioned before, in our school we have four academic teachers; which means that we teach multiple subjects. Currently, I and my colleagues, each teach seven different classes per day, (in the beginning it was eight). That equals 35 lesson preps per week, per teacher, in a full five day week. If you will also recall, I said that, in the beginning, we started this program with nothing more than the furniture in the rooms, no textbooks. No textbooks meant that we had to develop lessons ourselves.

Since I was still in university, I was accustomed to creating lesson plans. I had to create projects multiple times on a weekly basis for a grade. In a way, this was sort of a perfect scenario for me; because my lesson plans were critiqued by professionals. In my university classes, we were also asked to present our plans sometimes. So, not only did I get critiqued, but, I was able to pick up useful tidbits that I might be able to incorporate in some of my classes from my fellow teachers-in-the-making.

I have textbooks now, but, creating the lectures and worksheets myself is second nature to me. I rarely tell my students to, "Read Chapter 12 and do the questions at the end of the chapter." I like lecturing and having them to take notes. The time I spend writing their notes (and, sometimes drawing pictures) on the board is my time to gauge their understanding, answer their questions, engage them in discussion, and some story-telling. It's my time to bond with them, teacher to class. It's my time to prove to them that it's okay to ask questions, express opinions, even fantasize and explore the 'what ifs…' that may arise.

I'm not sure where the idea for this activity came from, but, I have been doing it for many years. It's one of my favorites, and I have found it to be very successful over the years. The majority of my students have a good time with this activity. It is Cinquain Poetry incorporating my little twist. It gives my students an opportunity to get their creative juices flowing, and it gives them a break from the usual drills of lectures and worksheets.

**Cinquain Poetry**

1. The first line consists of one word (Noun)
2. The second line consists of two words (adjectives)
3. The third line consists of three words (action verbs)
4. The fourth line consists of four words (a complete sentence)
5. The fifth and last line consists of one word (synonym of the noun from line one)

**Find the mistakes!**

Frog
Funky warts
Making foggy sounds
Lovely madly slimy green
Prince

Rain
Damp grass
Lonely misty trees
Lost in thoughts of you.
Empty

**Directions:** You must create three poems. Cut-out pictures from the nature magazines that you have used for your inspiration.

Mount the pictures on a piece of colored cardstock (one for each poem). You must use two Ecology vocabulary terms in each poem.

**Rubric:** Two points for each line—five points for each vocab term times two = 15 points per poem.

The Cinquain Poetry project is a versatile lesson. Not only does it reinforce the science skill of correctly using ecology terms, but, it combines a literacy lesson with the parts of speech.

I do not assign this project until after my students have had plenty of exposure, and practice using the Ecology vocabulary list that consists of approximately thirty terms. Then, when I introduce this project, we review the parts of speech and the tenets of a complete sentence. Next we "Find the mistakes" in the 'Frog' and 'Rain' poems as a whole group, in order, to check for understanding. I then share a correctly written piece of poetry (mine), with a picture of a waterfall, mounted on a piece of colored cardstock, as an example:

Water
Powerful fluid
Flooding Quenching Calming
Abiotic necessary to biotic.
$H_2O$

I see no reason the Cinquain Poetry activity couldn't be incorporated across-the-curriculum. I think it would be great to use for a particular time in history, event, or a country in geography. I even played around with a math theme, and came up with the following:

Algebra
Fair Balanced

Adding Subtracting Multiplying
Making the unknown known.
Expression

When the poetry is completed, I will ask each of them to pick their favorite from among their creations. I will then post their picks in the hallway for a few days for the other teachers and students to read. Some of them will put up a token pretense of embarrassment of having their work posted; but, I have caught the same students pointing out their work to friends in between classes, and explaining the process of Cinquain Poetry. I'm always astounded by the creativity of some of my students.

During my early years, I had a student who was very bright, and I would describe him as having a good heart. He was somewhat quiet, and perhaps a bit withdrawn. Although he was friendly enough with his peers, he usually kept to himself. He always had terrific input during classroom discussions. He wasn't overly talkative, but he could make his point with flair. However, trying to get him to do the standard, worksheet kind of lessons, without an argument, was nearly impossible.

One day, after a lively discussion, that he had taken part in; I gave the class an ordinary paper and pencil follow-up ecology assignment; he did his usual, and zoned-out. Feeling frustrated, I approached him and quietly told him he needed to do some of the work. I went on to say that he was just too smart to flunk-out. I explained that I needed something to grade, some tangible proof that he was as capable as I knew him to be. He said, "Let me write a song about the environment instead of doing the worksheets for a few days. I'll even bring my guitar and perform it for the class." I was quite surprised by this turn of events. I had never had a student to make such a suggestion before. I didn't want to discourage him, so, I agreed to his proposal with the understanding that I would need to see some physical proof that he was working on a song. Within a couple of weeks, he declared he was done and that he was ready to perform the song whenever I gave him the go-ahead. We picked a day, and true to his word, he brought his guitar to school, along with his neatly handwritten lyrics. He performed his song for our class, and later for all of the students, and staff in the cafeteria. He had woven several of the environmental concepts that we had discussed in his lyrics. His words were elegant enough for the most ardent of tree-huggers. I was so proud of him. As you might expect, he earned an 'A' for his work, and I learned the critical lesson of flexibility. Afterwards I framed the poetry that he had set to his original music and proudly displayed it in my room. As the year progressed, he did enough of the more mundane work to pass my class. I think I will always remember my troubadour.

Another lesson that I do with my students is from a non-traditional English class that I created. The focus of the course is on the basics. Identifying parts of a sentence, correct use of articles, some grammar, and poetry study. However, the majority of poetry is actually song lyrics. It is the hook I use to get them interested. It is my understanding that although my degree and certifications are in Biology and General Science; in an alternative setting one can teach any subject as long as one is a certified teacher. The lesson that I really enjoy teaching, and many of my students enjoy writing are metaphors. Hidden messages, a little mystery, seeking clues, and solving for a solution all seem to hold an appeal for most people. I start my metaphor unit by handing out and reading a short piece entitled:

## The Dress

*Every day I think about the dress. Not just any dress, but, the dress. It truly is a big decision; after all, it can, and probably will change my whole life... if I buy it. It has a very hefty price tag, and I will no doubt have to have it altered. After the alterations, it won't fit anyone but me. I certainly can't return it ad I can't give it away. I will have to sacrifice a lot in order to buy it...not just me but my family. It will be a considerable commitment to own the dress.*

*What will people think when they see me wearing the dress? I just know some people will think I'm too old to wear that style. But, then again, I've never been the kind of person to let other people influence my decisions. Not really important decisions...like buying this dress. Besides, I find myself daydreaming about the dress. I imagine myself wearing it. I can just see myself now....walking, standing, sitting...wearing the dress. It really could be perfect for me.*

*I think about the feel of the fabric and the way it will fit. Oh yeah, that's another thing I have to think about, the fit. What if, I mean really, what if; I buy it, have it altered and I don't like it? I will have wasted all that money and time if I don't wear it. Sometimes I wish I had never seen that dress!*

*Really, it has become an obsession for me. It's not as if I don't have other dresses; but, I'm tired of them. I have worn some of them for so long. Some of them I haven't worn in ages. But, nothing in my closet can compare with that dress.*

*How will it make me feel when I have it on? Will I feel as good about myself as I envision? I see others wearing a similar version of it. They splurged, they bought it. However, while some of them seem very happy in it, I have seen some looking absolutely miserable while wearing it; as if, they can't wait to take it off. I do not want to be like that; so unhappy in the dress that I make myself and everyone around me miserable. Decisions, decisions.*

*What is the worst thing that can happen? I will spend a lot of money and not like to wear the dress. What is the best thing that can happen? I will spend a lot of money, love the dress, and the dress will change my life in significant ways. Either way, I will own the dress.*

---

After reading the piece, I ask my students to share their thoughts about the meaning of the story. Nearly 100 percent will say it is about a wedding dress. I will then tell them it isn't about a dress at all. It is a metaphor; 'the dress' represents something else.

We will then review the differences between a metaphor, a simile, and an analogy. After, a few more guesses, I tell them that I wrote "The Dress." It is a metaphor for my decision to start college at the age of 37, to be a teacher. They will now go back to the handout and find the comparisons between buying an expensive dress, having it altered, being happy with it, and the decision to go to college to become a teacher. We compare the expense of college to the expense of a designer dress. The tailoring needed for a dress to fit correctly, and the selection of courses to complete my chosen academic major. We discuss the possible reactions people might have, due to my age, to the style of dress chosen, and my choice of starting a new career; particularly one that requires so much schooling. Lastly, we talk about whether or not I'm happy with my dress. The story and the follow-up discussion allows for further bonding and rapport building between myself and my students.

All of this is a precursor to their assignment of writing their own metaphor. In my class, the project is worth 70 points. I also have an alternative method for my non-writers, with a maximum point value of 50 points out of 70 points. The alternative method will be using an organization chart for their metaphor. I have supplied an example at the back of this book. Sometimes, the variance in the maximum point value will get them to re-think their choice of method. I explain to them that the students that choose to write an essay rather than filling in an organizational chart will put forth more work, and the extra work should be rewarded. I have never had any arguments. Regardless, of the method they choose, the metaphor must have a minimum of five comparisons. For those students that choose to do the chart, they have to explain the connections privately to me, or I will give them the floor to share with the class if they like.

I have had students that have written several pages revealing their innermost thoughts and their aspirations through metaphor. On the other hand, I have had students to use the purchase of a piece of clothing as a metaphor for the purchase of a vehicle. These are the students that usually go for the chart.

# 15 Making Choices

I'm not sure that I chose to work with At-Risk students. I made a choice to teach. I made a choice to work, to get my foot-in-the-door. But, I didn't set out to teach At-Risk students. When I decided to become a teacher I never gave any thought of being an At-Risk teacher; I imagined myself in an ordinary classroom. Actually, I pictured myself in an ordinary American History classroom. Two sessions into my university Biology classes and the picture shifted. I was hooked. I went to the front office while on a break during my second Biology class to inquire about the steps I needed to take, in order, to switch my major from Social Studies to Biology. I didn't plan to spend 18 years (with at least two more years to go) of my life teaching Biology to At-Risk teens, but, here I am.

---

"...Yet knowing how way leads on to way,
I doubted if I should ever come back...."
—Robert Frost

I am not going to go into a discussion on the nuances of Robert Frost's poem *The Road Not Taken*. But, I will borrow a couple of lines from the third stanza that I feel describes a part of my journey to becoming an at-risk teacher, regardless of the 'true meaning' of the poem.

As the poem goes, "...way leads on to way..." other teachers told me that by accepting the teaching position in the alternative school, my chances of my ever coming back to the point of choice again was highly unlikely.

I was told, "If you can handle working with At-Risk students with any success, odds are you will never get into a mainstream classroom. Even if you do succeed in moving from At-Risk to the mainstream; you may still find your rosters loaded with students that need extra attention; because you have proven that you can handle it." It had happened to one of the teachers that gave me the warning.

I have decided there must be some truth in their reasoning. Had I not proven that as a para I could handle it? And since I could handle it as a para; was I not offered a teaching position in an alternative setting before I had completed my certification? You know how an actor can be type-cast into a particular kind of role? That also happens in the world of academia.

But, sometimes we don't realize what we need until we get it. I grew up in a time when the Peace Corps was first introduced. Its' ubiquitous slogan "The hardest job you'll ever love" is a fitting description of my feelings about the path that I found myself on, within my profession. It has been hard. It has taken an emotional toll on me; and if I'm honest, my family as well. As with most jobs, we carry our day home with us. Those emotional ups and downs are not like a pair of shoes. We can't just pull off the day's events, and leave them at the back door when we get home. More than once, my husband has come home and found me in an emotional mess. More than once, he has held me as I cried for a student.

However, even though the lows may drag me to their depths, the highs will have me soaring. Those times when I have finally made a connection with a student. When a child that usually stares at the floor when speaking, finally makes eye-contact with me. When a painfully shy student, one that has been diagnosed with social anxiety disorder speaks out in my class for the first time. When a student that was ready to drop-out, comes to us, completes their paper chase, and walks across the stage in May to receive their high school diploma; that is a high that will have me soaring. At that time, I have received my ultimate professional reward. Fortunately, more than once, my husband has also celebrated with me when I brag of my students' successes.

I was forewarned that I would probably never teach in a mainstream classroom. To be honest, I have never tried. I never have put-in for a transfer. I have never applied in a different district; for one thing, your reputation will travel with you. I have never tried for a mainstream classroom, because, I have never felt an urge to be anything other than what I am now. An At-Risk teacher, teaching the sciences. I may not have chosen to be an At-Risk teacher in the beginning, but, it is my choice now. I have found my niche. It is a hard job, and I have loved it.

Remember in the beginning, when I said I wished for a wild and wonderful ride that was never dull? Well, I got it.

Metaphor Diagram

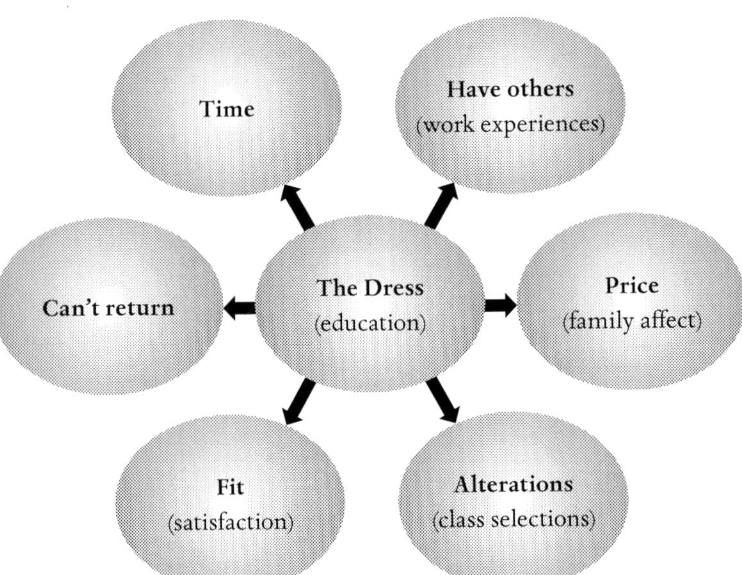

# In Conclusion

I would like to say, Thank you, for reading my book. It is my hope that after reading this book you will have gained a little insight into the At-Risk student. I hope I have, perhaps, provided a few helpful tips. It is also, my hope, to have given you a reference to understanding the teachers that deal with these unique children on a daily basis.

From the front cover to the back, every word written is my life, as an at-risk teacher, purely from my perspective, and observations of the past 20 years plus. And, although this book will never be considered a great tome, it is a representation of my legacy in my profession. During the writing process, I uncovered some old memories… good and bad. It has allowed me to do some soul searching, and to gain some perspective.

Maybe now I can now lay some of the bad memories to rest, and let the good ones flourish; because I have to go to work tomorrow to make more memories.

Printed in the United States
By Bookmasters